"Redekop's analysis is a timely and informative discussion of church-state relations. Those who recognize that both church and state are established and guided by God will find this book to be an important asset in assisting them in harmonizing their relationship with each institution in a principled fashion."
—*Vic Toews, Minister of Justice and Attorney General of Canada*

"This book is the fruit of a lifetime of service to Mennonite churches in Canada and the United States—and a lifetime of thoughtful reflection on the relationship between Mennonite faith and politics. There is much wisdom here. I will plan to use it in my teaching."
—*Ted Koontz, Associated Mennonite Biblical Seminary*

"John Redekop has insightfully articulated the interdependence of church and state. *Politics Under God* is a stimulating and provocative book. Lectures on these topics were warmly received by both religious and political leaders in the Democratic Republic of Congo. I highly recommend this timely and very helpful book."
—*Nzash Lumeya, Mennonite Brethren Church in the Democratic Republic of Congo*

"This bold reevaluation of the oft-competing claims of church and state and the Christian's role in each is sure to provoke much discussion. Redekop's Anabaptist heritage and wealth of experience as professor and sought after political commentator eminently qualify him to challenge our assumptions about the role that people of faith can and should play in a rapidly changing world. This analysis also casts a refreshing new perspective on the biblical directive that Christians be 'in this world but not of this world.'

"This book is a must read for those who struggle to reconcile the tension between the demands of faith and government yet desire lives that are relevant and that engage our communities on the issues that really count."
—*Ed Fast, Member of Parliament, Ottawa*

"John Redekop knows his subject, both as an academician and as a practitioner. He writes for followers of Jesus who need to come to terms with the church-state problematic and offers a reformed Anabaptist view that is positive about government generally. He is clear and balanced as he offers guidelines for involvement. In challenging long-held views he is provocative; in some circles he will be

controversial. I highly commend the book especially for group discussion as a way of sorting out the confusions in the tangled labyrinth of policy-making and politics."
—*Elmer A. Martens, Mennonite Brethren Biblical Seminary*

"John Redekop's life-time of writing and lecturing on these issues and his exceptional gift for communicating complex ideas and basic truths in an easy-to-understand manner come together in this book. The result is a harvest of helpful guidance for Christians who are politically active, be it as elected representatives, appointed officials, voters, taxpayers, or as people who pray for those in government."
—*William Janzen, Mennonite Central Committee Canada*

"John Redekop is a superb political scientist who understands the Canadian religious community from his many years in senior leadership. *Politics Under God* is a masterful synopsis of the constantly asked question, 'What does Christian faith have to do with politics?' This book is foundational on the subject, and there is no better place to begin searching out that question. What an enormous service Redekop has done for us. Bravo!"
—*Brian C. Stiller, Tyndale University College and Seminary*

"John Redekop draws masterfully on Scripture, theology, history, and the social sciences in making a passionate and reasoned plea for evangelicals to participate in the political process and thereby have an impact on the social contexts in which they find themselves. Beyond theology and theory, Redekop spells out tangible ways in which Christians can be part of that process. This is an important book that makes a clear case for why politics cannot be ignored by any evangelical who aspires to have an influence on personal and collective life."
—*Reginald Bibby, University of Lethbridge*

"Drawing on his extensive experience as an academic, professor, church leader, and political activist, John Redekop provides a timely and passionate primer on politics, citizenship, and the relationship between church and state from a Christian perspective. Whether or not you agree with his 'Anabaptist realist' approach, you will find this book packed with practical and helpful insights into our Christian responsibility to bear a constructive witness to governments."
—*Bruce Clemenger, Evangelical Fellowship of Canada*

Politics *Under* God

Politics *Under*
God

John H. Redekop

Foreword by John A. Lapp

Herald Press
Waterloo, Ontario
Scottdale, Pennsylvania

Library and Archives Canada Cataloging in Publication
Redekop, John H. (John Harold), 1932-
    Politics under God / by John H. Redekop.

ISBN 978-0-8361-9355-8
    1. Christianity and politics—Anabaptists. 2. Church and
state. 3. Christianity and politics. I. Title.
BX4935.P64R43 2006   261.7   C2006-904440-6

POLITICS UNDER GOD
Copyright © 2007 by Herald Press, Scottdale, Pa. 15683
    Published simultaneously in Canada by Herald Press,
    Waterloo, Ont. N2L 6H7. All rights reserved
Library of Congress Catalog Card Number: 2006931714
Canadiana Entry Number: C2006-904440-6
International Standard Book Number (10): 0-8361-9355-5
International Standard Book Number (13): 978-0-8361-9355-8
Printed in the United States of America
Book design by Sandra Johnson
Cover by Greg Yoder

12 11 10 09 08 07 06   10 9 8 7 6 5 4 3 2 1

To order or request information, please call
1-800-759-4447 (individuals); 1-800-245-7894 (trade).
Web site: www.heraldpress.com

To all Christian politicians
who have served God and humanity
by promoting justice, decency, compassion, freedom
and respect for human dignity.

Contents

Foreword

I RECOGNIZED JOHN H. REDEKOP as a kindred spirit after reading his first book, *The Christian Far Right*, in 1968. Both of us shared an intense interest in the world of politics and wanted to understand how those of us committed to a narrative of peace, justice, and service can engage a world obsessed with a narrative of national greatness. Both of us were interested in demonstrating, as Redekop wrote in 1972, "that mature Christianity should lead to political sensitivity and subsequent activity." Since 1968 our paths have occasionally crossed while sharing a platform or committee table. Kindred spirits may not always agree, but they point in the same direction.

Redekop speaks out of a Canadian context with frequent references to other national contexts. His experience of politics under God has been quite congenial. Nonetheless, his critique of the Christian far right already in the 1960s highlighted the dangerous character of a political ideology rooted in Christian nationalism: today all sides of the current conflicts in the Middle East frequently appear inspired and sanctioned by religious authorities, even within presumably secular societies.

Redekop also speaks out of that part of the Mennonite tradition that has been more ready than other groups to participate in political activity at the national level. His sisters and brothers among the Mennonite Brethren are now dealing with the interesting phenomena of being in communion with part of the family of the president of Paraguay. Indeed all Mennonites active in Paraguayan public life are demonstrating considerable creativity in the conversation between the narratives of church and state.

Politics Under God represents the mature insight of a well-trained political scientist and a deeply committed church leader. (Redekop is perhaps the first Mennonite scholar with a PhD in political science.) Each chapter deals with a topic or question that is intrinsic to Christian practices in public life. Redekop recognizes differences among a variety of Christian traditions but always circles back to Anabaptist points of view as interpreted by many modern Mennonites. His opening chapter on politics as seen in the Scriptures is referred to again in an appendix of relevant texts.

I found the chapter "What Does God Require of Governments?" especially insightful. The "twenty God-pleasing tasks" are worth frequent referencing in the vital political processes of any jurisdiction—local, national, international. Some but not all of these are referenced in the chapter "What Does God Require of Christian Citizens?"

As I read these pages, I was struck by their relevance these very days. Guest columnist Roger Scruton wrote in the *Wall Street Journal* on August 17, 2006, that western Christians and Jews are "heirs to a long tradition of secular government" that believes "human societies should be governed by human laws, and these laws must take precedence over religious edicts. The primary duty of citizens is to obey the state. . . . All religions must bow down to the sovereign authority if they are to exist within its jurisdiction." Redekop's attention to separation of church and state is a timely reminder how churches have dealt with such a political philosophy for twenty centuries.

The day after Scruton's column appeared, *New York Times* reporter Howard French wrote in considerable detail the story of authorities destroying an almost completed church building in eastern China. The lawyer for this unregistered church group observed that the authorities "are afraid of the Christians and don't want to see Christianity develop." *Politics Under God* from beginning to end highlights the value of religious freedom and provides a frame of reference for a response.

Politics Under God is meant to be applied. As such, readers will adapt Redekop to their own situation and may also raise new questions. I hope individuals will find groups with which to explore the issues further in their own settings.

Redekop highlights the formal rather than the informal dimensions of politics. The roles of political parties, the media, and popular education are significant for creating the climate for political activity. The author could have demonstrated how Christian disciples need one another in order to discern the shape of attitudes and actions for political life. Sometimes those from outside one's national situation see things more clearly than those on the inside. Struggling to hear their voices is essential in a worldwide church. He has an excellent analysis in chapter 10 of liberal, conservative, and socialist points of view, but could have given more attention to those forces that create political consciousness.

This volume should be considered a basic text for Christian disciples who want to shape their politics with a consciousness of the reign of God.

—*John A. Lapp*

Acknowledgments

THE PREPARATION OF A MANUSCRIPT requires not only disciplined thought and appropriate writing by the author but also the input of many other people. For encouragement, motivation, and in some cases assistance in preparing this volume I thank Nzash Lumeya, Abe Dueck, Elmer Martens, and the late John Howard Yoder. At Herald Press, Levi Miller and Michael Degan played major roles in bringing this volume to completion. My wife, Doris, deserves special recognition not only for her encouragement and constant support but also for assistance in various secretarial and research tasks.

Numerous Christian politicians and statesmen have influenced me greatly over the years. These include former U.S. Senator Mark Hatfield and former Canadian Members of Parliament Robert Thompson, Jake Epp, and Tommy Douglas. With all these distinguished leaders I have had substantial interaction. Former U.S. president Jimmy Carter has been an important role model by demonstrating how one can bring Christian ethics to bear in policymaking at the highest levels of government. In some respects former U.S. President Reagan also drew upon Christian ethics in shaping policies.

A special word of thanks goes to the many thousands of students I have taught over the years, many of whom have pressed me hard to reconcile a conservative Christian faith commitment with the realities of government, an agency established by God and which functions as his servant. This book constitutes a small step in advancing dialogue and discussion about that challenging agenda.

—John H. Redekop
Abbotsford, British Columbia
October 9, 2006, Canadian Thanksgiving Day

Introduction

EVERY CHRISTIAN EXPLANATION of church-state relations rests on certain assumptions about both the church and the state. It incorporates a particular understanding of what the Bible says about both. Not surprisingly, libraries are filled with competing explanations. The discussion has a long history.

In the early 300s, following centuries of persecution of Christians, Emperor Constantine embraced Christianity and affirmed it as an important ally of the state. Later in the fourth century, Emperor Theodosius declared Christianity to be the only true religion. He made it the state religion and branded followers of all other religions as heretics. In the early fifth century, St. Augustine, in *The City of God,* rejected theocracy but nonetheless argued that any state that wanted to pursue justice must include God's norms in its laws or it would be nothing but a large-scale robber band. In the thirteenth century, Thomas Aquinas argued in his *Summa Theologica* that although the inclusion of Christian virtues made for better laws and greater justice, fallen humanity could, by relying on God-given natural abilities, achieve satisfactory political organization without consciously including Christian virtues. He argued that this goal had, after all, been achieved in some communities long before the advent of Christianity.

During the Reformation of the sixteenth century, Martin Luther asserted that "temporal authority" must necessarily function according to an ethic lower than the Christian ethic but that civil government was ordained by God to uphold civil law and keep evil in check. Both "regiments," church and state, were established and guided by God, and Christians had a duty to serve not only in the church but also in political offices. Writing in the *Institutes,* John Calvin, Luther's contemporary, went a step further. Like Luther, he affirmed the two orders, the political and the spiritual, but added the assertion that a truly good government would take direction from the church and serve it as much as possible. The church was thus given a superior role in church-state relations.

While Luther and Calvin were still advocating that church membership and citizenship should not be separated, the Anabaptists, led by Conrad Grebel and Menno Simons, advocated a departure from past assumptions and practices. They were seen as radicals for asserting that church and state should be separate and insisting that full religious freedom is biblically mandated. Let me add at this point that the Anabaptist interpretation is given fairly extensive treatment in this volume, because I deem it to be the closest to the New Testament teaching and therefore the one to which I subscribe.

An important and distinctive perspective has been advanced by a distinguished Mennonite theologian, the late John Howard Yoder. In *The Christian Witness to the State* and *The Politics of Jesus,* this Anabaptist scholar has spelled out a radical approach. He describes what he sees as the political irrelevance of Christian pacifism, he denounces all "modern war," and he advocates the minimization of any political involvement. Interestingly, he also urges Christians to express a strong witness to the state. He further encourages the cultivation of a political advisory role for certain faithful Christians, because some actions are wrong not only for Christians but also for the state. He adds that although the political powers function according to unchristian ethics, they do carry out an "ordering function" and can be used by God for some good purposes. We need to acknowledge at this point that Yoder's focus was on witnessing to political authorities rather than on the potential positive aspects of politics or on participation by Christians in the political arena. Even so, it seems fair to say that Yoder held a rather low view of politics as an arena for Christian service.

In more recent times we encounter many other interpretations of church-state relations and many prescriptions of how Christians should relate to the political realm. In various countries, certain leaders have championed so-called Christian nationalism, a fusion of the cause of the church with the cause of their particular country. Christian-Americanism is a case in point. At the other end of the spectrum, groups such as Americans United for Separation of Church and State want to remove even the slightest trace of religious, especially Christian, presence from the governmental realm. And, of course, the Hutterites and some very conservative Mennonite groups attempt total withdrawal from all things political.

While obviously gleaning insights from these and other sources, the perspective presented in this volume rests on a perhaps unusual understanding of Scriptural teaching about church-state relations and a fairly optimistic view of governmental structures when compared to its alternative, anarchy. It could be termed "Anabaptist realism." As readers will see, it posits the faithful church as consisting of committed Christians giving overriding allegiance to God and his kingdom, and it views the church as having an ethic and a purpose far above anything that can be associated with the political order. But such an assertion need not, in this perspective, view the state as something evil or describe it as the enemy of the church. Rather, the state is seen as something much more positive, an agency affirmed by Jesus and the New Testament writers.

The fundamental assumption in this analysis, which is presented as being rooted in Scripture, is that both the church and the state have been established by God. Both are expressions of his divine love. For the church, this love is expressed in profound and intimate ways as the love of the Lord for his bride, the people who have accepted the divine plan of salvation and the lordship of Christ. In political terms this relationship encompasses theocracy. We might term this expression of love and the resulting relationship of humanity to God as God's perfect plan, God's Plan A.

Unfortunately, most of God's human creatures have not responded positively to God's plan of salvation and discipleship. Either they have not heard about it or they have heard it and rejected it. Many millions have gone their own defiant way. But God, the ultimate expression of love, did not abandon them. While respecting their God-given freedom of choice, which since the garden of Eden has included the right to choose wrongly and reject God's lordship, God nevertheless extended his love to such people by providing political structures for them. Such provision by God can be termed God's Plan B. By and large these political structures, even when autocratic, have served humanity well. As Yoder reminded us long ago, "even tyranny is better than chaos."[1]

It can be argued that this expression of divine love by the establishment of political structures has its genesis in God's commandment concerning the "mark of Cain" (see Genesis 4:15) and has benefited most of humanity for thousands of years. Viewed thus we can say that the political order has actually had a much longer history than the Christian church has had, although the concept of the "people of God" goes back to the book of Genesis and perhaps to creation itself.

We should note that some scholars see the establishment of government as part of creation and point to the fact that God mandated Adam "to have dominion . . . over every living thing" (Genesis 1:28 KJV) and invited him to name all the animals (see Genesis 2:19). This view rests on a definition of government that is very broad. If we accept it, then we need to develop another term to describe what is commonly referred to as government. Having dominion over plants and animals is not, in my view, a political responsibility; animals are not governed. Neither is the responsibility to name animals a political activity. Governing relates to people. Politics has to do with polity, by which we mean an organization of human beings for temporal and not religious purposes to achieve certain goals, such as establishing and maintaining a peaceful and stable society. I do not see the establishment of human government as part of God's creation as recorded in the first two chapters of the book of Genesis.

Although God has established both the church and the political order, they necessarily function according to different norms. We will illustrate and analyze some of these differences. Since Christians live in both realms, as citizens in the political realm and as Christian disciples in the church, tensions and challenges arise. Two systems of ethics seem to be involved. Luther, and to some extent Calvin, lodged the two ethics in one person. This approach creates huge inconsistencies. The early Anabaptists adopted what strikes me as a more biblical stance—the notion that a person can ultimately embrace only one ethic. Whatever the view, there will be tensions. This book suggests by what means many of the resulting challenges can be processed. A fundamental guideline is that in politics as in any other societal pursuit, including business, organized labor, the various professions and vocations, Christians should get involved only to the extent that Christian discipleship permits. The standard should be consistent and applicable to all callings.

Readers will note that I emphasize the notions of "conservative Christianity" and "conservative Christians." While there are obviously other important categories, I stress these for three reasons. First, this category encompasses all believers who accept Scripture as the inspired word of God with applicability to all areas of life. They thus take biblical ethics as normative. Years ago I asked a friend if he accepted the Bible as being inspired. He said that he did, that the Bible was inspired "just like Shakespeare is inspired." Conservative Christians hold to a narrower definition, one with clearer boundaries and with convictions that dictate behavior and facilitate analysis. Second, I focus on this category of Christians because that is the one to which I belong. I thus analyze issues that are basic in my own life. And third, I deal with this group because I deem it to be the most consequential one. If one does not have a high view of Scripture, it is difficult to sharpen the issues of agreement and disagreement between political and Christian perspectives. I might add that while the views of other Christian groups are important, and we can doubtless learn much from their stances toward the political realm, space limitations do not allow me to deal with them in this slim volume.

Some readers will surely find my analysis of the political realm as a general category to be surprisingly positive. Some will find my affirmation of governments and description of citizenship responsibilities unusual for an Anabaptist believer. To them and to all readers I would say this: Test my analysis carefully. Are my statements true to Scripture? Are my observations and suggestions too time-bound? Are they too situation-specific? Are they tied too closely to the workings of a free and open democracy? Is my analysis of the biblical texts in line with the historical Anabaptist view of Scripture? A biblically based analysis of political reality should, after all, be applicable to all situations and should incorporate a defensible interpretation of the key biblical texts. To the extent that the following chapters fail to meet such standards, revision is required.

The issues and challenges raised in the following chapters will, I suggest, become increasingly important in the coming years. Throughout most of the world, governments are expanding in scope and in policy claims. The results are both positive and negative. In many jurisdictions these activities, even if rooted in a sub-Christian ethic, create major opportunities for participation by Christian citizens and, concerning some vital issues, even the organized church as a whole. In some lands, even in democratic societies, these claims and actions impact the church in negative ways. Sadly, in many countries, political pressures against the church are truly tragic and have produced not only restrictions and harassment but also prosecution and large-scale persecution. Such governments have abandoned God's intention for them. They need to be reminded of their ultimate accountability to the King of kings.

The purpose of this book is threefold. First, it introduces readers to what I see as the key issues in church-state relations. Second, it provides some practical suggestions and guidelines for Christian citizens who take both their faith and their citizenship seriously. And third, this analysis illustrates, at least in an introductory manner, a perspective about church-state relations that I term Anabaptist realism.

The church-state relationship is a complex one in both theology and political studies. It is also complex in actual practice. The political realm presents some opportunities but also some major challenges and serious dangers. While both church and state are agents of God, it is the church, not the state, that is the bearer of the meaning of history; it is the church, not the state, that deserves primary allegiance; and it is the church, not the state, that will ultimately prevail.

1

Biblical Guidelines Concerning Church-State Relations

To be a follower of Jesus involves two decisions: first, to accept the salvation Jesus offers and second, to live a life of obedient discipleship. Throughout the history of the church, followers of Jesus have had difficulty deciding how obedient discipleship should express itself in the realm of politics. The challenge is still with us whether we live in a dictatorship, an oppressed colony, a country struggling to establish itself as a viable state, or in a free and democratic society. Christians face many challenges and choices whether we live in a country at war or a country at peace, and whether we live in a country ruled by military forces, by an authoritarian clique, or by a democratically elected government.

At the outset we need to clarify some terms. As used in this volume, *politics* refers to activity related to governments, including the actions of public officeholders, of those seeking to become officeholders, and of political parties and other organizations seeking to place candidates in government positions. This includes voting and other citizen involvement, whether in political parties or not, that relates to the selection of public officeholders. Equally political is all our activity intended to influence government policies and actions, whether we seek exemptions and privileges for ourselves or justice for others. And when we speak of governments or public officeholders, we speak of the authorities who govern any political jurisdiction, be it a city, a state or province, or an entire country.

While all organizations have officeholders, that is, people with leadership responsibilities, governmental officeholders differ from others in that only they have the last word, the final authority, in their realm of responsibility. Governments are distinctive because only they have the authority and the power to regulate and control all other organizations in the area for which they are responsible. Only governments have such power. As some writers put it, only governments exercise the authoritative allocation of resources and only governments establish official policies.

In any stable society, then, only governments have the power to enforce their policies not only by persuasion and education but also by fines and imprisonments and ultimately by control over life itself. Although many governments do not employ this ultimate power, only governments can practice capital punishment and, concerning external affairs, employ military might. To point to this fact does not, I must stress, constitute an endorsement of either capital punishment or a declaration of war. This police and military power exists, whether it is not used at all or whether it is used only in a limited manner, or only in crisis times, or very widely as in a brutal dictatorship. In other words, political power is distinctive because government is the only power center that potentially or actually controls and sets the guidelines for all other power centers in its realm, ranging from the family and school to business corporations and labor unions. It should be noted, of course, that in federal systems this power is shared by two levels of government, the national and the provincial or state level. The country's constitution spells out which level gets which power. Very limited power is typically also delegated to cities and municipalities.

In free societies, of course, governments greatly limit their potential control of citizens and organizations, but they never give up the potential power to control citizens and organizations. That is what distinguishes governments from all other organizations.

We sometimes speak of politics in business, of politics in labor organizations, and even of politics in the church. It may be useful to speak in these terms, but technically it is not correct. These other organizations have only very limited power, only such power as the state allows them to exercise. Concerning physical coercion these organizations possess only such authority as has been granted them by the governments in their area. They do not possess ultimate legal coercive power.

Political Involvement by Christians

We turn now to the question of political involvement. While some Christians stress the truth of Philippians 3:20 that "our citizenship is in heaven" and urge avoidance of any political involvement as described above, other believers spell out reasons we should take political matters very seriously. The major ones can be summarized as follows:

- The Bible addresses this matter and provides some fundamental guidelines. See, for example, Romans 13:1-7; 1 Timothy 2:1-4; 1 Peter 2:13-17; Acts 16:37-39; Acts 5:25-29; Romans 12:2; Matthew 22:17-21; and Hebrews 12:14. These biblical passages will be discussed in detail later.
- No part of our life lies outside the scope of Christ's lordship. Christians must bring Christ's teachings to bear on all areas of life. "All the world," as indicated in Mark 16:15, allows for no exceptions of either geography or society. No people

and no structures escape God's care, concern, or judgment.

- Most of us are greatly affected by political matters and are much more involved in politics than we may realize. Even the attempts to avoid political involvement do not eliminate people's political significance. Ultimately, the issue is not whether to be involved politically but how to be involved politically.

- The impact of political affairs on the life of the Christian church is increasing markedly. In part this reality is caused by the expanding role of governments in most countries. This trend holds true almost universally in democracies as well as in nondemocratic countries.

- If the proper functioning of government is a divine mandate, then we have a responsibility to understand this arena, to increase our knowledge, and to improve the quality of our participation. Government, after all, was "established by God" and is "God's servant" (Romans 13:1,4).

- Even a cursory survey of history, including recent times, demonstrates that while many Christians have shown great insight, many others have made huge mistakes in reacting to and dealing with political realities. Throughout the past millennia, many so-called "Christian" governments have actually behaved in totally unchristian ways. We ought to learn from those who acted wisely as well as from those who did not. We should not repeat the mistakes of the past. Rather, we should build on the many fine contributions made by faithful Christians over the centuries.

A person's perspective makes a big difference in how one reacts to the political environment. Permit me to summarize some of my views based on more than forty years of experience, observation, teaching, and research. New understanding and additional light are, of course, always sought and always welcome.

1. Christians must learn to take politics seriously without giving politics the status of ultimate seriousness.
2. Most Christians, I suggest, either underestimate or overestimate the capacity of government for remedying evils in society or facilitating progress.
3. Both the state and the church tend to make absolutist claims; for the Christian, only the cause of Christ can make valid ultimate claims.
4. Many Christians are confused about the role of government in God's scheme of the world. Unless we are clear on the basics, our attitudes and our actions may be inconsistent and even contradict our Christian beliefs.
5. Let us never try to limit the ways in which God may choose to work and may wish to use us, even in political arenas. It was God who selected Joseph, Daniel, and others for special political roles. Let us always seek to understand how God wishes his followers to serve him in the broad realm of political activity.
6. Christians need to resist the temptation to become chaplains, in a fundamental and unqualified sense, to sub-Christian governments and agencies. Sometimes we need to disturb consciences rather than calm them. Any chaplaincy must therefore be selective and qualified. We ought always to be ready, of course, to minister to the needs of any person.
7. Historically the state has often evoked almost blind support, even among Christians. This reality runs counter to the transnational, in fact global, nature of the church. Many people, including Christians, seem more willing to die for their country than for their faith. Christians need to ask why this is the case.
8. Appropriate Christian involvement in politics can strengthen a person's Christian witness; it can reinforce our saltiness, our expression of love to others (see Matthew 5:13).
9. Christians ought to balance two praiseworthy emphases: *social activism* (the Old Testament prophets; Jesus driv-

ing the moneychangers from the temple, and so on) and *withdrawal* ("Therefore come out from them and be separate," 2 Corinthians 6:17). The best outcome is selective involvement.

10. For a Christian the church and the cause of Christ are always primary while the state and the claims of government are always secondary.

11. The state is not in itself evil. Although it functions at a sub-Christian ethical level, it is a mixture of good and evil. Much of what governments do is praiseworthy. This fact should not be surprising given that in many countries many of the state's activities were pioneered by the church.

12. Faithful Christians have a constant gadfly function in society; governments should always be challenged to do better. Because it operates at a sub-Christian level, the state cannot be trusted to decide by itself what it should do and what belongs to Caesar.

13. Unless the claims of Christ dictate otherwise, as in Acts 4:18-21, where civil disobedience was required, Christians are called to be model citizens, living according to high moral standards.

14. During the past millennia, Christians have disagreed over where to draw the line concerning political involvement. Some have sought very extensive, we might say even dangerous, cooperation of church and state. Others have sought almost total noninvolvement in the political realm. Our basic stance should be to respect all choices but also to evaluate each according to the claims of Christ and biblical ethics.

To those who are inclined to seek extensive involvement we say that Christians should pursue any activity only to the extent that Christian discipleship permits. To those who seek avoidance of all political involvement, even to the point of not voting, we say that political significance and relevance cannot be avoided. As, for example, during the time when Hitler and his associates launched the Holocaust, silence and inaction by most Christians also spoke volumes. It is a myth to think that we can escape politics. We do acknowledge, of course, that there is a major ethical difference between intended consequences of our involvement and the unintended consequences of our noninvolvement. Our accountability for the former is much greater than our accountability for the latter.

Instituting Government

We turn now to the question of how the institution of government came into existence. God did not initially create the civil order, the order of state and government. He created only one order or kingdom, the one existing in the garden of Eden and of which he was the only sovereign and ruler. When God announced that creation had been completed, as recorded in Genesis 2:2, there was no political order as we understand the term. There was only theocracy—God-rule.

God's granting of free moral choice did, however, give rise to the political order. By allowing his human creatures the choice of obeying him or turning against him and rejecting his lordship, God made possible the emergence of a society that made wrong choices and went its own way. Such choices began early in human history with the wrongful action of Cain. Perhaps it began even earlier, shortly after the creation, with the first instance of disobedience by both Eve and Adam. In any event, when mankind, whose free will God does not violate, rejected God's plan and guidance, God, in his mercy, did not abandon them but established a new order.

This new order, the political order, began when God "put a mark on Cain so that no one who found him would kill him" (Genesis 4:15). Thus God began to establish rules for those who rejected his complete lordship. People would not be permitted to take the law into their own hands. There was

to be no anarchy; the rule of law was to prevail. Cain was to
be protected from personal vengeance or mob rule. God did
not permit lynching! This, then, is the beginning of the civil
or political order. God later prescribed many rules and procedures, always respecting the people's right to make wrong
choices. Of course, at times he also punished entire nations
for making wrong moral choices.

Beginning with the mark of Cain, God thus provided
structures that would enable even an ungodly or sub-
Christian society to function. The political order can therefore be seen as God's Plan B, a second-best arrangement, an
expression of the fact that until the end of the age God never
abandons his human creation to their own evil ways.

It might be argued that this establishment of a civil order
was a special arrangement that God made for his own people, the Israelites. That the establishment of a civil order has
broader validity is confirmed by Jesus' statements in the
Gospels. For example, with reference to the Roman Caesar,
totally anti-Christian in his values, Jesus asserted that his followers should nevertheless pay taxes to Caesar and the occu-
pying Roman authorities. He further bestowed legitimacy on
that government by saying, in response to the Pharisees'
attempt to trap him, "Give to Caesar what is Caesar's, and to
God what is God's" (Matthew 22:21).

Given the above, as well as the significant emphasis placed
on secular governments by Paul and Peter (Romans 13:1-7;
1 Timothy 2:1-3; 1 Peter 2:13-17; Titus 3:1-2), it is clear that
Christians should submit to governments, pray for governments, pay taxes to governments, and be thankful for governments. In Romans 13 we read that not only has God instituted
government as his "servant" to "punish evildoers" and "do you
good," but also that Christians should submit to government,
pay their taxes, and honor those who govern. In 1 Timothy 2:1-
2, Paul says, "I urge, then, first of all, that requests, prayers,
intercession and thanksgiving be made for everyone—for kings

and all those in authority." Such clear and straightforward directives were given to believers who lived not in a democracy but in an oppressive, totalitarian empire. How can any Christian set aside that which is to be "first of all"?

Christians need to acknowledge that while secular governments are outside the perfection of Christ, they are not outside the perfection of God's love. Governments function outside the realm of redemption but not outside the realm of God's concern and compassion. This results from the fact that God's love extends to all those who make wrong moral and spiritual choices, in fact, to all who reject him. Further, God always deals with disobedient or wayward people, even his own chosen people, at the place to which their disappointing exercise of free moral choice has brought them. That, for example, is why he assisted the children of Israel in the selection of their first king, the tall Saul, even though their demand to have a human king was fundamentally wrong and greatly displeased him (see 1 Samuel 8–10.)

While governments are not part of God's redeemed kingdom, God nevertheless has a specific mandate for governments as spelled out in Romans 13 and elsewhere. This mandate has both positive and negative components. Stated briefly, governments are to restrain evil, reward the good, promote freedom, and generally function in a manner that enables people to live in peace and enables the church to be about its more important business, namely, carrying out the great commission. Governments thus facilitate the carrying out of the great commission even though they may be quite unaware of having such a role.

In summary we can say that God did not create the civil order but that, beginning with the mark of Cain, he facilitated its development. God did not create the two realms, but man, exercising his God-given free will, brought it about.

Christian Citizenship

Since all Christians now find themselves living in two realms—the church, which is the order of Christ, and the state, which is the political order—it is important that we spell out some basic realities about Christian citizenship. Although Christians in various traditions have taken differing views, the following observations deserve serious thought.

Christian citizenship is part of Christian discipleship. It is part of living consistently, responsibly, and obediently in a sinful society. While discipleship must never be fused, or confused, with good citizenship, it certainly should transform it just as much as it transforms all other aspects and dimensions of living. The ethical guidelines in our citizenship activities are exactly the same as for all other arenas of our involvement, including business, education, management, labor unions, the various professions, farming, and any other honorable pursuit undertaken by Christians. In politics, as in all other areas of life, Christians practice loving servanthood and, having decided to get involved, do so only to the extent that Christian discipleship permits.

For a Christian, citizenship activities are always secondary and always conditional. Obedience to Christ and his teaching is primary. Christian citizens take the realm of government very seriously, just as Jesus did, but they never give it the status of ultimate seriousness. Christian citizens are known as obedient and law-abiding people, but they do not obey any government directives that violate God's requirements.

Another reason Christian citizenship is always conditional is that the church of Jesus Christ is not attached to any one government, country, or political ideology. When the church is faithful and consistent, then from God's perspective it knows no national boundaries or ethnic exclusion. There is neither Jew nor Greek, Congolese nor Angolan, Canadian nor American, black nor white. Its members, constituting an organic body, are citizens of many lands. They are grateful for their countries and for the existence of governments rather than anarchy, but they do not give ultimate or unconditional allegiance to any country.

Given linguistic and cultural diversity, as well as major differences in political systems and regulations, Christians tend to organize in local, regional, and national associations. Distances, mountains, deserts, and oceans also play a part. However, such differentiation is a functional arrangement, one of convenience and efficiency. The transnational unity of the Christian church always transcends all functional divisions. When nationalistic attachment becomes strong, the acceptance of this reality may be difficult for some Christians, but it is God's requirement. All Christians are sisters and brothers in the Lord before we are citizens of any given country. If large numbers of Christians throughout the world really came to understand this basic truth and to live accordingly, there would be much less warfare, because Christians would not be fighting one another, they would not be trying to kill one another in order to uphold the honor and well-being of their various countries. In God's kingdom, family ties trump patriotism!

Members of the church know that they are mere sojourners on earth. Christians may be inclined to sing the national songs of their temporal kingdoms and republics, especially if they are democratic and free, but they know that their most important anthem is the song of the King of kings and Lord of lords. They take their citizenship responsibilities and opportunities seriously, but they hold to no earthly allegiance that would override their divine "sonship."

Christian citizenship incorporates the biblical imperative to do good to all people, to express love and compassion in all areas of life. Christian citizens, therefore, look for areas of ministry in the political realm. At least some of us believe that there is a public or political equivalent to giving someone a cup of cold water (see Matthew 10:42). We agree with a key statement adopted by the International Congress on

World Evangelism in Lausanne, Switzerland, in 1974: "that evangelism and socio-political involvement are both part of our Christian duty."

Such an inclusive view of doing good to others means, for example, that our stewardship concerns do not end with reference to payment of taxes when we have parted with our money. We desire to see good deeds carried out by governmental authorities, who gather and then redistribute, on our behalf, a substantial part of our income. According to Romans 13:4, that is precisely what God expects governments to do. Therefore, as we have opportunity, we try to influence the wise use of tax revenues. In fact, in a functioning democracy, where we elect governments, we share some responsibility for what is decided. Similarly, we are concerned about governmental and private-sector treatment of the physical earth about which we claim to have important stewardship responsibilities.

In some countries Christian citizens find that the agendas of the faithful church and of governments overlap to a considerable extent. Such a situation should not be surprising, because in many instances government agendas consist of doing that which the more sensitive Christian community has pioneered. These areas include many categories of education, many dimensions of healthcare, provision for the handicapped, support for the elderly, caring for orphans, providing food for the hungry, and offering international aid.

Throughout church history, some Christian groups have taken a contrasting view of Christian citizenship. Certain groups, such as the Hutterites and some conservative Mennonites, have tried hard to avoid any involvement in the political order. They still hold such views today. They deserve respect, for they too are making an important Christian and political statement. They are carrying on the avoidance, perhaps also the suspicion, of government that characterized some Mennonite groups in Switzerland shortly after the

Reformation. Some early Mennonites, it seems, saw the political realm as essentially evil. In the Schleitheim Confession of 1527, the drafters of the document referred to the political order as the kingdom of "darkness." For them, living in a time of brutal persecution and under a government that performed hardly any positive tasks, such an assessment is understandable. But in my view the Schleitheim Confession is too negative. Jesus would not have asked us to pray for the government or to pay taxes to it, to obey it and to be thankful for it if it were intrinsically evil.

Even those of us who have a fairly optimistic understanding of Christian citizenship and hold to an inclusive definition of doing good deeds readily acknowledge the existence of some basic tensions between the two orders. Enlightened political behavior, at its best, is guided by the principle of justice. Christian behavior at its best is guided by the law of love. Stable political life depends on compromise, a meeting in the middle where that is ethically justifiable. The pressures to compromise will create some tensions, given that mature Christian living is guided in many areas by absolute notions of what is true and right.

Consider the following contrasts. The primary guiding commitment for a national government, the guardian of the state, is self-preservation. The overarching, guiding commitment for Christians is obedience to God. In secular political life, status, popularity, power, and control are held in high esteem; in the Christian life, servanthood, submission, sacrifice, love, and worship of God are most important. As we have seen, there is considerable overlap of enlightened political agendas and certain Christian ministries, but we must not ignore the basic differences. The tensions are real.

Conclusion

In concluding this introductory survey, permit me to list some general observations.

1. The political realm is very important but it must not become the major concern of the church.

2. In the political realm, as in all other pursuits, we do not all have the same gifts or calling. We need to allow for considerable diversity and greatly differing levels of involvement. We need to allow for a Joseph and a Daniel but also for those who limit their political agenda to prayer and intercession as required by Scripture. Prayer for governments, we remind ourselves, is not optional.

3. Christians must always resist the temptation to use government power as a short cut to try to achieve Christian behavior or belief. Becoming a Christian and living the Christian life involve voluntary commitment, not external conformity compelled by outside coercion. Of course, some Christian ethical principles have such obvious validity and utility that they have been enacted into law by governments.

4. A sub-Christian society, even an enlightened one, can be made more just, more humane, and more civilized than it already is, even though it does not explicitly accept Christian ethics. There are various levels of sub-Christian ethics, ranging from the depravity of Nazism and Stalinist Communism to the enlightened policies of many democratic countries in our time.

5. Any Christian citizen who is concerned enough about the political order to pray for it, as the New Testament commands us to do, should also seek to be informed about it and, if possible, should challenge what is blatantly evil and support what is obviously good. Such responses can be undertaken personally, collectively, or channeled through the various Christian organizations that regularly relate to policymakers. Prayer is not a substitute for positive action. Rather, it is an associated undertaking.

6. In most countries, the Christian church is of a sufficient size that it cannot be irrelevant. Even if silent, it sends a strong message.

7. Despite the many sad chapters in its history, the state remains an important expression of God's providence and love. Even when officeholders of the day are corrupt and evil, and even when we work to remove and replace them, Christians thank God for the existence of political structures instead of anarchy.

8. While the political order has done much that is good, it is the church, not the state, that is the bearer of the meaning of history. God has called the church, not the state or any political government, to be his messenger proclaiming his gospel.

2

Theological Perspectives on Church-State Relations

THE QUESTION OF HOW the Christian church should relate to political authorities has been with us a long time. In fact, one can trace political problems back to the time of Jesus, even to the time of his birth. It was, after all, the political ruler, King Herod, who wanted to kill the infant Jesus (see Matthew 2:16-18). Later it was another political ruler, governor Pontius Pilate, who gave permission for the crucifixion of our Lord. After the church was established, great persecution was initiated by other political authorities. The challenges of church-state relations have been with us ever since.

In virtually every country in modern times, the arena of church-state relations has included a broad range of issues. Depending on the country, the following questions have been central: Will the government grant religious freedom to Christians? Will the government try to ban or suppress Christian or other religious activities? Will the government accept religious pluralism in the country's population? Will the government grant religious freedom to minority religions? Will the government try to make one religion a state religion? Will there be discrimination against Christians?

Will the government discriminate against minority faith groups? Will the government allow one religious group to persecute some other religious group? Will the government be willing to cooperate with faith groups where the two have overlapping or common agendas? Will the government respect Christian and other conscientious objectors? And to what extent, if at all, should Christians cooperate with government?

Christian understanding of what constitutes correct church-state relations has varied markedly. The fact of the matter is that people read and understand the biblical texts differently. In this analysis, we review several major interpretations. This very brief survey will not only help us to understand why certain historical church-state relationships have occurred, but should also help us to evaluate the options and to develop our own views more fully.

In describing these options we must note that the main emphasis is placed on the classical formulations. In later centuries, although the core emphases remained, many refinements and variations have occurred.

The Catholic Church and Church-State Relations

The dominant church-state tradition since the late fourth century is the Roman Catholic one. For the first three centuries the Christian church was generally harassed and periodically persecuted brutally by imperial Rome. As late as AD 303, an exceptionally antagonistic policy was carried out when Emperor Diocletian ordered all Christian churches destroyed, all Christian scriptures confiscated, and all bishops and lesser clergy tortured and killed unless they sacrificed to Caesar's image. At first with vigor and later more sporadically, this policy was carried out in many parts of the Roman Empire.

The situation changed drastically in 313 when Emperor Constantine granted full religious freedom to Christians in the part of the Roman Empire that he controlled. In 323 he

became the sole ruler of the empire and extended his enlightened policies to additional territories. Not only did he restore
all lost properties to the church, he also made the Christian
Sunday a legal holiday throughout the empire and ordered
many churches built. By 383 Christianity was declared the
imperial state religion by Emperor Theodosius I. While such a
policy may have been courageous, it should not be seen as beneficial for the faithful church. The church does not depend on
or use the arm of the law to carry out the great commission. For
centuries thereafter, the Roman church enjoyed supremacy.
Unfortunately, biblically-based freedom was eroded. Working
in partnership with imperial Rome, the church gradually suppressed all dissenting sects and set guidelines for much of
daily life for all citizens.

Although the Roman Empire weakened in the late fourth
and early fifth centuries and was eventually defeated, the
church continued in its role of supremacy. Even when political leaders in various parts of Europe challenged its dominance, it generally retained its control in Europe and beyond
until challenged massively by the Protestant Reformation in
the early part of the sixteenth century. The key point to keep
in mind is this. For more than a thousand years the Roman
Catholic Church dominated life in Europe to the point that
for most of the time, most political rulers were subordinate
to it.

At the heart of the traditional Roman Catholic view is
the assumption that the ecclesiastical authorities possess a
moral authority over political institutions. Is that assumption
still held by the Roman Catholic Church? Is that still the
ideal arrangement from a Roman Catholic perspective? That
point is in dispute among Roman Catholic ecclesiastical leaders and scholars. In any event, today, partly because of internal revisionist thinking and partly because of the emergence
of independent countries in most of the world, the Roman
Catholic Church enjoys absolute control in only one little

state, the official center of the church itself, the Vatican, located in Rome. In other countries it has gradually lost or yielded its absolute power over political authority, although in some countries, in parts of Latin America for example, it still influences and perhaps even shapes much of the governmental process.

Reviewing history, some scholars say that apparently the ideal church-state relationship from the Roman Catholic perspective is "church over state." The church should be superior to the state because it has a higher moral authority. If this moral assumption is valid, does the church thereby gain the right to make political decisions or to at least lord it over the political authorities? Does the church thereby possess the right to define moral standards, be it on the basis of natural law or divine revelation, for all of society? Does the church possess the right to set the limits of religious freedom and restriction? One can find apologists who argue that it should do so.

Reform Catholics, a growing sector of the church, would state the matter differently. They argue that the Roman Catholic Church, despite its God-given understanding of moral law, should no longer try to impose its will on political authorities. Generally speaking, the Roman Catholic Church in most countries no longer tries to do so. Reform Catholics also state that the Roman Catholic Church should support religious freedom and not try to suppress other faiths. In many countries the Roman Catholic Church now adheres to such policies.

Church and State—A Lutheran Perspective

While in the last several centuries Lutheran teaching in this area has undergone important diversification and reform, most of the basic emphases developed by Martin Luther are still embraced by most Lutherans. Therefore, we do well to spell out the classical Lutheran understanding as set forth by the great reformer himself. We will study this perspective in some detail because of its dominant position in Protestantism to this day.

Martin Luther's central theme concerning church-state relations is that God exercises divine sovereignty over all aspects of human existence, including the political order. To bring about his will on earth, God uses Christians as well as non-Christians, and he does so in working through the "two regiments," or two kingdoms—church and state. Luther reminds us that Jesus himself spoke of the kingdom of God and the kingdom of this world. Both kingdoms are subject to the rule of God and both are objects of his love and wrath.

Luther defined the Christian regiment, the kingdom of God, as consisting of all true believers in Christ. If they were thoroughly Christian and living by themselves, he asserted, they would need no secular law, sword, or ruler. In contrast, the worldly regiment is a consequence of sin. It consists of all other people. It is not morally self-sufficient and needs a government: "All who are not Christians belong to the kingdom of the world and are under the law." People in the worldly kingdom are "subjected to the sword so that they [unregenerate sinners] cannot practice their wickedness."[1] Although in his theology Luther also allowed for sin in the kingdom of God, in his explanation of the need for government, he seems to overlook that fact. Further, although Luther tried hard to define the two kingdoms as separate entities, he was forced to acknowledge that in practice the functioning of the "kingdom of the world" actually included all people. This situation existed partly because very few people were thoroughly Christian in their behavior and partly because much of governmental activity necessarily impacted Christians as well as others. Such an acknowledgment obviously weakened his dualistic classification of people.

Luther asserted that God, in his infinite wisdom, has established two agencies—the state and the church—through which he governs his two kingdoms. The state relies on law and the sword to keep the peace, to keep sin within limits, and to promote civic righteousness. The church relies on the Word, on love and humility, on persuasion and, ultimately, excommunication and the ban. Its mandate is to convince people of sin, to proclaim the good news of justification by faith, to help people attain everlasting life, and to facilitate growth in Christian discipleship.

Unlike the basic Roman Catholic distinction between a lower order, the realm of nature, and the higher order, the realm of grace, Luther's two realms, the realm of law and the realm of gospel, are almost equally significant arenas of God's activity. The two regiments share a divine source and divine mandate but differ in function. Because it relates to the eternal state of souls, the church is given greater emphasis and is more significant.

Each regiment can help the other. The state provides orderly conditions so that the church can do its work. The church helps the state by furnishing citizens who are pious, submissive, pay their taxes, and honor their governments. (Citizens who are not Christians must also obey their governments, although they probably do so out of fear.) Neither regiment should use the methods of the other nor interfere with the activity of the other. God uses both regiments in his continuing battle against evil and the devil until God's ultimate triumph over Satan. Accordingly, when Christians obediently support governments in their efforts to counter evil, they strengthen God's hand against the devil himself.

Given that both regiments further God's will, Christians are called to serve in both regiments; both types of service constitute "Christian vocation," or calling. Both kinds of service involve the expression of Christian love, although such love takes on almost opposite forms when expressed in the church and when expressed in the political arena.

At this point Luther encountered a fundamental problem. He insisted that Jesus' ethic applies to all Christians, and he also acknowledged that worldly governments have to rely on the sword, something not permitted in Christ's church. He tried to resolve this dilemma by arguing that when Christians serve in the worldly regiment, and when as obedient citizens they may even have to kill, they do so "in a spirit of love."[2] He even went so far as to assert Christian citizens may have to kill in order to preserve the political state.[3]

Relying on this peculiar understanding of Christian love in action, Luther insisted that political officials, no matter what they presumably have to do because of their offices, can be good Christians. He developed two lines of argument. First, since God is using the state to punish the wicked and defend the good, a Christian's service in government or the military is a divine service to God. After all, society could not survive if there were no one willing to arrest and execute criminals and defend the country. God's purpose would be thwarted if Christian citizens would not help to preserve the state. Second, when Christians wield political power, punish evildoers, execute criminals, and fight in wars, they do so not for their own good, not for themselves, but out of concern for their neighbors. Such actions, when done for the common good and not for oneself, become "works of love." They are expressions of love for one's neighbor.

Luther realized, of course, that the political and military actions he was praising contradict Jesus' Sermon on the Mount, but he argued that they nevertheless become works of love when done because one holds a political or military office. The office, apart from the officeholder, has its own ethical standard. What would otherwise be evil can become good because of the "office" or position one holds when carrying out the action. Christians should therefore "leap at the opportunity" to serve God in political and military roles. Luther wrote:

> Therefore, should you see that there is a lack of hang-
> men, beadles, judges, lords, or princes, and find that you

are qualified, you should offer your services and seek the place, that necessary government may by no means be despised and become inefficient or perish. For the world cannot and dare not dispense with it.[4]

From this perspective, the strong ethical norms Jesus taught in the Sermon on the Mount apply only in matters of personal interest. They do not apply in the public sector.

While Luther was no great supporter of war, he believed that war is a legitimate activity for both the ruler and the subject if undertaken to preserve the political regiment, an agent of God. Although Christians do not defend themselves, he argued, they do aid rulers in defending the given political realm.

In Luther's view, a war for national protection and self-defense is a just war. It is the ruler's responsibility to decide when war becomes necessary. It is the citizen's responsibility, whether Christian or non-Christian, to fight if called upon to do so. Luther wrote that it is "a Christian act and an act of love confidently to kill, rob, and pillage the enemy, and to do everything that can injure him until [one's ruler] has conquered him according to the methods of war."[5] Interestingly, Luther also asserted that when a prince wrongly undertakes a war, his Christian citizens should not follow him, for they must obey God rather than man.[6] Clearly this qualification created a huge problem for Christian citizens. It seems to me that Luther's basic stance was this. Otherwise unchristian acts become Christian if undertaken to support a ruler in a just war; otherwise unchristian acts continue to be unchristian if undertaken to support a ruler in an unjust war.

Despite some important insights that Luther brought to the problem of church-state relations, several serious weaknesses in the Lutheran perspective must be faced. First, his distinction between "spiritual" and "temporal" kingdoms is too simplistic. The church, too, has temporal aspects. It possesses power and can misuse it. Further, a Christian citizen does not function in only one regiment but lives and functions in both. Luther acknowledged this obvious fact but gave it relatively short shrift. The sharp citizenship distinction Luther drew, especially in some of his writings, is both unrealistic and misleading.

Second, Luther assumes that blatantly unchristian acts can become Christian if one has the right motive, a motive rooted in so-called political necessity, and especially if one holds the right office, a political office. Not surprisingly, he cites no biblical justification for such a view. With such a mindset, one could rationalize away almost any evil action undertaken by political authorities! "To kill in love," as an expression of Christian discipleship, stretches credulity. In addition, of course, we must deal with the questions of who determines political necessity and how anyone can prevent self-serving and aggressive action being justified as political necessity.

Third, Luther's explanation of ethics creates a huge problem. Can a person really lead an integrated life under Christ's lordship if he must always be asking himself, "Am I doing this as a Christian or as a citizen?" Can a Christian separate his Christian identity from his identity as a citizen? Further, can a Christian always know in which of those roles he is doing something? Even more problematic, can he maintain within himself two quite opposite ethical modes of behavior, a contradictory ethical dualism, without sacrificing integrity? Is the result not some sort of ethical schizophrenia? And can a Christian function effectively if he must always be preoccupied with ethical gear shifting?

Fourth, does the average Christian citizen possess the ability to understand and calculate which war is just and which is not? It boggles the mind to assume such a capacity, either in our day of complex, puzzling, and obscure foreign and domestic policy interests or in Luther's day, when the average person was generally uneducated, illiterate, and ill informed. And what would a ruler likely do if some of his soldiers suddenly decided that the current war is unjust? Would they become the enemy?

Fifth, Luther's notion of the "just war," widely held even to this day, creates many additional problems. Historical evidence demonstrates that blame for a war rarely lies solely on one side and that almost any war has been and can be justified by all sides. Luther's explanation also justifies situations, all too common in warfare, in which Christians line up in battle on opposite sides and try to kill one another. For example, millions upon millions of Catholics and Protestants did this in World Wars I and II. My mind cannot affirm the idea that the church of Jesus Christ, the global body of redeemed believers, should act that way. Can God be pleased if Christians train their guns and bombs on one another and do their utmost to kill fellow Christians, all in the name of Christian citizenship duties?

In sum, the classical Lutheran perspective on church-state relations, which at least in its ethical essentials is perhaps the dominant view among both mainline and evangelical denominations today, leaves much to be desired as a consistent and biblically rooted prescription for Christian citizens.

The "Reformed" Understanding—a Calvinist Perspective

This perspective is sometimes called theocracy because of its emphasis on God transforming all aspects of his creation. In some key respects it is similar to Lutheranism, but there are important differences.

Whereas Luther stressed the separation of the two regiments and attributed to the government only a limited capacity for true justice, John Calvin saw all of society as a *corpus christianum,* a much more unified whole, an inclusive Christian body, so to speak. "Christ as head of his church is also precisely the Lord of this world."[7] Gone is the sharp distinction between the Christian order and the non-Christian order. Calvin stressed the Christian role of the state and asserted that its function is to help Christians live the Christian life. Luther gave only the church a role in man's redemption. Calvin, while still differentiating between the functions of church and state, also gives the state a christological, salvation purpose. In this respect he harks back to some extent to a more medieval Catholicism in which all of life and society is unified under the cross.

Although in Calvin's scheme the church does not control the state, it comes close to doing so by claiming the right to decide which dimensions of life should be governed by the church and which by the state. Concerning the state's role, Calvin asserted that "The civil government . . . should act in terms of the will of God, seeking in God's Word how best the political order could contribute to the salvation of its citizens, as well as providing an orderly and beneficial temporal setting for their daily life."[8] In God's providence "civil government is designed, as long as we live in this world, to cherish and support the external worship of God, to preserve the pure doctrine of religion, to defend the constitution of the church."[9] Beginning in 1536, Calvin sought to establish such a system in the city of Geneva, Switzerland.

In Calvin's Geneva, the church had great freedom not only in matters of doctrine and rigorous church discipline; it also had state-delegated authority to carry out rather harsh ecclesiastical punishment. Moreover, the church expected the state to help carry out the church's mission, which included the punishment of those who were spiritually wayward. Not surprisingly, over time the functional distinction between the church and the city government in Geneva became blurred. For example, on issues such as the election of elders, the appointment of ministers, and the control of church finances, "the political authorities held decisive power."[10] The church, however, never gave up the right of excommunication.

In Calvin's Reformed system, the "civil order," that is, the city council in Geneva, should suppress idolatry, blasphemy, and sacrilege because "this civil government is designed, as long as we live in this world, to cherish and support the external worship of God, to preserve the pure doctrine of religion, to defend the constitution of the church."[11] Calvin argued that "no government can be happily constituted, unless its first object be the promotion of piety, and that all laws are preposterous which neglect the claims of God and merely provide for the interests of men."[12] Thus, although Calvin believed in the existence of two independent authorities under God, in this form of theocracy the distinction between the two realms became blurred, if not obscure, after he finished describing what they each should do.

This problem came to a head in Geneva when Calvin tried to use the consistory, a senior church committee composed of ministers and laymen, to decide the values and rules by which a society should live. Although the consistory itself undertook only to reprimand and excommunicate the wayward, it proceeded to blur the distinction between the two sets of authorities by referring political offenders for additional temporal punishment. Thus a sinner/criminal in Geneva was subjected to both spiritual and temporal penalties. Before long, the state was actually executing religious dissenters for the church. It may be too simplistic to say that Calvin established a dictatorial church-state union in Geneva, but it's not far from the truth.

On the questions of war and the political activity of Christians, Calvin generally agreed with Luther. He also agreed with Luther on the ethical distinction between the office and the person holding it. Accordingly, concerning this aspect Calvinism is necessarily subject to the same criticisms we spelled out with reference to classical Lutheranism. Because of the additional role that Calvin assigned to government, he was even stronger than Luther in arguing that to resist political authorities, except in extreme situations, is to resist God. He argued that even when so-called unjust rulers practice brutal rule, subjects should not rail or revolt but rather acknowledge that God is using a cruel ruler to punish sins.

To a considerable extent, then, the evaluation of Calvinism parallels the evaluation of Lutheranism, although on some issues we can identify differences.

First, it is significant that neither Luther nor Calvin utilized the logic we described above when assessing an invader or deciding if a war is just. Neither allowed for the possibility that God was using one country, perhaps even an evil country as in Old Testament times, to punish another country, even Israel, his own chosen nation. Further, concerning citizenship duties, as Thomas G. Sanders puts it, Calvin "fell into the same sort of ambivalence between the divine and the demonic as Luther, taxing the Christian with the problem of deciding whether he should self-critically accept travail as a form of God's punishment, or oppose it as a travesty of God's intentions."[13]

Second, by utilizing the political authorities to inflict temporal, often extreme, punishment for presumed sins or unacceptable beliefs in the religious realm, Calvin obscured the distinction between sin and crime and went far beyond the responsibilities the New Testament assigns to the state as well as to the church.

Third, most contemporary Christians would surely argue that it was never intended that political authorities, who might themselves not even be Christians, carry out church discipline.

Fourth, in Calvin's scheme, there is no place for religious freedom, religious dissent, or many other basic freedoms. Given the centrality of freedom in God's dealings with human beings, this shortcoming is crucial.

Fifth, the earlier criticisms of the classical Lutheran view of war and of the attempted distinction between office and officeholder, described above, obviously apply here as well.

Sixth, Calvin attaches too much worth to the merely external expressions of Christian behavior. Throughout Scripture, and particularly in the New Testament, the essence of true Christianity is defined as being internal. The language refers to heart, mind, and spirit.

Seventh, throughout Calvin's writings there seems to be an implication that one can and should expect substantial elements of Christian discipleship from people who are not Christian disciples. I see no biblical support for such a view. We have no biblical basis for assuming that God expects ungodly rulers to practice Christian discipleship, but we do know that God does expect enlightened and just governing by even ungodly rulers. We encounter this truth in the account of Babylon's King Belshazzar (Daniel 5:22-28).

Before leaving our analysis of the classical Calvinist perspective, I should say that in more modern times Presbyterians, various branches of the Reformed faith community, and other Calvinists have substantially moderated classical Calvinism. The harsh church-state rule of the Puritans under Cromwell in England (1649-60) and of the Puritans and Pilgrims in some New England settlements in colonial America, which harked back to Calvinist assumptions, is a thing of the past.

Calvinists today do not attempt to get political authorities to inflict religious punishment nor to undertake any other direct involvement in the church. Rather, they are concerned about getting governments to be as fair and as just as possible and to enact into law as many basic Christian principles as possible, always on the grounds that doing so would serve the entire population well. Nonetheless, the emphasis on all of society coming under the rule of God and that all people, including governments, should act "Christianly" remains strong. One might well ask, then, whether there is still too much blurring of the distinction between a lost world and the body of Christ.

Other Perspectives

Three additional perspectives deserve mention at this point. We turn first to the "separationist" understanding of church-state relations. In its modern version it is largely an American phenomenon of the past two centuries. In this view the idea that the church and state must be kept functionally separate is taken so far that even the slightest presence of Christian symbols or teaching in the political realm, including public education, must be opposed by true Christians. There must be no religious presence in the political order. The Lutheran and Calvinist dilemma of trying to have a population, or at least its pursuits, separated into strictly religious and strictly secular spheres arises here in a new guise. But this perspective trips over itself. Life cannot be so simplistically and decisively compartmentalized.

Second, in the Quaker understanding of church-state relations, especially in the last century, pacifism is dominant. In Quakerism there is very little concern about what happens to the security of the political realm or to the state itself. That is not the Christian's or the church's concern. Christians have no responsibility for the well-being or survival of any given political order. There is considerable concern, however, for the adoption of ethical policies by governments. While acknowledging and at times even emphasizing divine sovereignty over all of society and all political affairs, Quakers concentrate on being guided by the "Inner Light" in carrying out the great commission and functioning as the salt of the earth. Quakers, generally speaking, have taken very seriously their responsibility to witness to governments and, despite their pacifist bent, have developed an impressive tradition of political engagement.

The third option is that of the Anabaptists, including the major sector known as Mennonites. Although generally embracing pacifism, albeit with decreasing acceptance by many rank and file members, the Mennonite view, in contrast to the Quaker perspective, takes very seriously the preservation of the political order. It is held by most contemporary Anabaptists/Mennonites that the Christian church has much to say to government. In earlier times there was great reluctance to get directly involved in the political order; in more modern times involvement has become extensive. This option will be analyzed separately.

3

An Anabaptist/Mennonite Understanding of Church-State Relations

IN HIS ANALYSIS of the various concepts of church-state relations, Thomas G. Sanders writes, "Protestantism bears no stain more serious than the acquiescence and even encouragement of Luther, Zwingli, and Calvin in the persecution of these innocent fellow Christians by the 'sword' of the temporal authority."[1] While the numbers of Christians in the Anabaptist/Mennonite branch of the reformation in the early sixteenth century were not large, this often-misunderstood group was, nevertheless, distinctive and significant. Sanders' assessment is that "they more accurately reproduce the views of the New Testament church than any other perspectives toward the state under consideration here."[2]

The Radical Reformers
Several important traits of these "radical" reformers, led by Conrad Grebel, Menno Simons, and others, need to be noted at the outset.

First, their overarching desire and determination was to

revive pre-Constantinian New Testament principles. They rejected the entire medieval Roman Catholic perspective. They agreed with many of the theological reforms advocated by Martin Luther and John Calvin, but they categorically rejected others. They insisted that the so-called "great reformers" did not go far enough in theological doctrine and that they were in error in their prescriptions for church-state relations.

Second, in the early Anabaptist interpretation the political realm, expressed by the state, is seen as a mixture of good and evil but mostly evil. The early Anabaptists affirmed that the office of government is, indeed, ordained by God but emphasized that it originated because of sin and that Christians should refuse to hold any political office. In the Schleitheim Confession of 1527, as we have already noted, the political realm, since it is not part of God's kingdom, is seen as part of the kingdom "of darkness." Given the brutal sixteenth-century treatment of these courageous reformers by Catholics as well as by followers of Luther and Calvin, authorized by the rulers of the day, such a negative assessment is understandable.

Third, the early Anabaptists held a very high view of the Bible. They committed themselves to be guided by the teachings they found in it. Since they had no clergy class, the Scriptures were studied by an entire congregation or some smaller group for guidance in all the important areas of life.

Fourth, there were important differences within the movement. We will focus on the main, moderate group. Smaller, theologically related groups such as the militant, almost communistic Münsterites, the spiritualists and mystics led by Hans Denck and Sebastian Franck, and the communitarian Hutterites led by Jakob Hutter, adopted somewhat different views.

Theological Propositions of the Anabaptists

In their desire to recapture the key teachings of the New Testament church, the early Anabaptists spelled out a set of theological propositions that established the foundation for their view of life and society, including church-state relations. We now turn to their seven key propositions and assess the significance of each one.

First, the church of Jesus Christ consists of voluntary believers who become members on the basis of conversion and baptism on faith. Pedobaptism, the christening of infants, is not taught in Scripture. It does not constitute baptism and is of virtually no value. The infants are unaware of what is being done. Their will and commitment, let alone any expression of faith, are not involved.

The consequences of this theological assertion were far-reaching, especially when combined with the Anabaptists' rejection of the notion that baptism should be associated with citizenship. Gone was the insistence, expressed by both Martin Luther and John Calvin, that baptism and citizenship go together. Citizenship and church membership would now be unrelated. Also rejected was the idea that the general population should follow a ruler in the affirmation of the religious faith accepted and endorsed by him. The fundamental Anabaptist insistence on voluntarism sets that prescription aside.

Second, the basic Christian ethical teachings, as spelled out in the New Testament, especially in the Sermon on the Mount, are valid for all Christians and in all areas of life. The ethics enunciated by Jesus were not intended for only an elite or clergy class nor were they prescribed for some future age. The acceptance of this ethic is unconditional. All other ethical considerations flow from it.

Here, too, the social and political consequences were far-reaching. The Anabaptists rejected any notion that the followers of Jesus should live by two sets of ethics, as both Luther and Calvin taught, one governing their actions as Christians and the other governing their actions as citizens. They insisted that the New Testament does not teach such a duality. Jesus and the apostles taught only one ethic and it is valid for all Christians in all situations. If the demands of a particular role or vocation require some other ethic, then Christians should not be in that role or vocation. The early Anabaptists took the call to Christian discipleship so seriously that they did not permit any social or political considerations to condition their commitment to follow Jesus. The Anabaptists acknowledged that their standards were rigorous but they insisted that one could, in fact, function in accordance with these standards in any situation. An important precondition, of course, was that such a believer must be ready to die for the true faith.

The Anabaptist assertion that Martin Luther, John Calvin, Ulrich Zwingli, and their associates had not gone far enough in the areas of baptism, discipleship, and citizenship precipitated angry reaction by Luther and Calvin. Both urged their followers and the rulers of the day to arrest and, in many cases, to kill the Anabaptists. Many were burned at the stake. This brutal and widespread persecution by reformers who were themselves reacting to assorted evils carried out by the Roman Catholic Church in the name of Christianity is a tragic blot on the achievements of these supposedly great reformers.

Third, while the Anabaptists agreed with Luther in his emphasis on justification by faith, they differed with him by focusing mainly on discipleship, *Nachfolge,* rather than on a particular conversion experience. They did not reject the importance of such an experience nor did they minimize the centrality of justification by faith, but they insisted that the real test of any decision to accept Jesus as Savior is the willingness to follow him in discipleship. Luther saw salvation as the gift of a merciful God and wrote a polemic against works. The Anabaptists, while also affirming the role of grace and faith, saw a life of faithful Christian love and works as evidence of the new life in Christ.

Not surprisingly, with such an emphasis the Anabaptists found the major reformers and their followers seriously lacking in faithfully living the Christian life and following the Christian ethic in the areas of citizenship and church-state relations. How could one claim to be a Christian while committing obviously un-Christlike deeds and justifying such behavior on the grounds that the political office, not the person, was responsible for those deeds?

This basic question is, of course, still relevant for the bulk of mainstream Christians and evangelicals who still hold to Lutheran ethical dualism. Christian soldiers, I am repeatedly told, don't kill as Christians; they kill as citizens!

Fourth, the Christian church is fundamentally a community, a "brotherhood," with very important interpersonal ties and responsibilities. Christian discipleship, it follows, is also a corporate phenomenon, not only a matter of individualistic values and activities. This means that a congregation incorporates strong bonds of love, practices extensive mutual aid, and undertakes collective correction. Some Anabaptists took this idea so far as to establish a type of economic communitarian lifestyle that they based on the early example of the Jerusalem church, even though that experiment was less than successful. This general emphasis on the church as a voluntary community contradicted the reformers' retention of infant baptism.

Fifth, the New Testament, the Anabaptists argued, sets out a covenant theology. Christ, as the head of the church, has a covenant with his people. They viewed the Old Testament as spelling out a covenant for Israel but argued that for Christians the new covenant has superseded the old. The main significance of this assertion was that the ethic of the old covenant does not apply to Jesus' followers. People of God now claim a higher ethic. The Anabaptists based their case largely on Jesus' numerous statements in Matthew 5 when he set aside the old ethic and spelled out a new ethic. He stated, for example, "You have heard that it was said, 'Love your neighbor and hate your enemy.' But I tell you: Love your enemies and pray for those who persecute you" (Matthew 5:43-44).

This distinction between the two covenants had great consequence for an understanding of church-state relations. Under the Old Testament covenant, rulers and members of God's people could, in various situations, employ violence and warfare to achieve the desired religious goals. Under the new covenant, as understood by the Anabaptists, Jesus had set aside all reliance on coercion. The new covenant relied only on persuasion and voluntarism. The use of excommunication, the ban, and perhaps shunning was as far as the faithful church should go in punishing anybody. Luther and Calvin disagreed strongly on this point. Both used the strong arm of the law and coercion by local rulers to achieve compliance in religious matters.

Sixth, emphasizing Jesus' enunciation as the Prince of Peace, his extensive teaching about peace, his negative reaction when Peter drew a sword to try to defend Jesus, and the rest of the New Testament teaching on peace and nonresistance, the Anabaptists adopted a strong peace stance. Non-Christians might well draw the sword and fight in self-defense, but true believers should not do so. They would rather accept whatever the consequences might be. Nor would they take up arms in defense of the political realm. They spelled out two main reasons for not doing so: first, New Testament teaching did not allow them to kill others and, second, the claims of Jesus took precedence over any call or claim by political rulers.

Both Luther and Calvin predictably rejected this Anabaptist stance. In fact, some of the harshest, almost vitriolic, animosity one reads in Luther's writings was directed against the pacifism of the Anabaptists. Because he believed them to be both seditious and blasphemous, he urged that they be opposed, harassed, hunted down, and even killed.[3] Ulrich Zwingli and the Calvinist reformers held similar views. The governments of the day were inclined to accept the counsel of Luther and Zwingli. "In 1529 an imperial edict announced that 'every Anabaptist and rebaptized person, of whatever age or sex, [shall] be put to death by sword, or fire, or otherwise.'"[4]

Seventh, the faithful Christian church will be a suffering church. The early Anabaptists took Jesus' statement literally when he said, "Remember the words I spoke to you: 'No servant is greater than his master.' If they persecuted me, they will persecute you also" (John 15:20). Matthew 5:11-12 was of great comfort to them as by the thousands they were mercilessly persecuted for their faith—flogged, tortured, burned at the stake, buried alive, and drowned in rivers: "Blessed are you when people insult you, persecute you and falsely say all kinds of evil against you because of me. Rejoice and be glad, because great is your reward in heaven, for in the same way they persecuted the prophets who were before you."

Church-State Principles of the Anabaptists

On the basis of these fundamental theological assertions, the early Anabaptists developed a series of principles concerning church-state relations. While the emphasis on Scripture was basic, these reformers were also influenced by their experiences under largely despotic and brutal political regimes.

First, the Christian church, as a faithful body of believers, functions largely as an alternative society. Even when the faithful believers live among the unconverted, the faithful community is functionally and ethically distinct from the kingdoms of the world. Ethically, the church and non-Christian society are thus two separate entities. Society, through government, has certain valid claims on Christians, since they are also citizens in the earthly kingdom, but any governmental claims and commands are secondary and must be rejected if they conflict with what is required in the Christian community.

With such a stance, although derived from biblical study and not from political theorizing, the early Anabaptists became the first champions of the separation of church and state. Not rational arguments but their understanding of Christian discipleship brought them to such an amazing insight and such a consequential conclusion. Simultaneously, these much-despised "radicals" also became the first modern champions of religious freedom, freedom that, significantly, they claimed not only for themselves but also for all other people. This constituted another profound innovation.

Second, although it is established by God, the state exists primarily to maintain law and order among non-Christians and ranks far below the church in significance. It is at best a mixture of good and evil. God has no absolute norm for it. The state simply exists to serve humanity at a sub-Christian level of law and order. Love is not its ethic and being other-oriented is not its norm. The political order is an accommodation to the sin of the world; it relies on power and coercion, a requirement far removed from the Christian virtues of love, humility, and mercy. While not actually demonic, the state functions outside of the church in a realm where Satan has much sway. It is nevertheless a sign of God's providence, and the office of government is ordained by God and therefore deserves respect.

Third, although God ordained the political magistracy, Christians should not hold office in it. As Article VI of the 1527 Schleitheim Confession puts it, "The sword is ordained of God outside the perfection of Christ." In the worldly realm it may be necessary to use the sword, but Christians, if asked to serve in the magistracy, should reject it just as Christ did when the people wanted him to become their king. The reasoning was that the weapons in the worldly realm are carnal and "against the flesh only,"[5] while Christians' weapons are spiritual. Christians are armed with truth, righteousness, peace, faith and the Word of God. We have here a very radical dualism between the two, ethically unequal, orders established by God for the good of humanity.

Fourth, the Anabaptists acknowledged that some governments are worse than others. Some rulers persecuted them and killed them; others at least let them live! Although it is to be desired that rulers should be as fair, just, and enlightened as possible, God has no final or second-best set of ethics for the state or its agent, the government of the day. At whatever ethical level a government functions, Christian citizens should always urge it to be more enlightened, more just, and more God-pleasing.

Fifth, because of the strong emphasis on peace in the New Testament, the Anabaptists refused military service. They saw the use of the sword as contradicting the call to follow Jesus. In fact, they also asserted that the use of the sword was, in the final analysis, also not in the interests of the larger society.

On the question about whether governments are ever justified in going to war, the early Anabaptist literature is mostly silent. Some Anabaptists were critical of how the war against the Turks was being waged, and some expressed strong opinions about the conduct of the Peasants War. One can surmise, though, that since the use of the sword was assumed to be necessary in maintaining law and order in society, it would also be seen as necessary, albeit a necessary evil, in national defense.

Sixth, because the world is largely an evil place, the best option for followers of Jesus is to withdraw from the malaise as much as possible, to be a separated people even in a physical sense where that can be done. They did not want their presence, their resources, and even their marginal participation to enhance a ruler's political and military power. Nor did they want to take advantage of whatever opportunities might exist to pressure rulers to be more enlightened. They did not see such action as their Christian duty. Admittedly, perhaps such avoidance and withdrawal might result in even greater governmental evil than would otherwise have been the case, but they would not be responsible for it. They insisted that they had drawn the line in such a place that they would be ethically distanced from the consequences of actions by evil rulers.

Given such a mindset, many Anabaptists sought to be "the quiet in the land." They would be grateful for whatever enlightened policies governments might follow and also accept, if necessary, whatever oppressive actions the rulers might inflict on them. Accordingly, for many of them farming held much appeal and although initially most were craftspeople in towns and cities, large numbers took up agricultural pursuits.

What do we make of this classical Anabaptist understanding of church-state relations? Many scholars and other observers have praised these radical reformers for their biblicism, their consistency, and their willingness to die for their faith. Their stance has aptly been described as "Christian life without compromise." Their emphasis on peace, in a world often torn apart by war, has also been praised, albeit sometimes grudgingly. The emphasis on mutual assistance and love for one's enemy has similarly evoked respect and affirmation.

Not surprisingly, there have also been major criticisms of this view of church-state relations. It has been argued, for example, that this view expresses relatively little concern for the social ills plaguing non-Christians. Non-Christians, too, are neighbors of Christians. They, too, are to be the object of Christian love and compassion. Further, it has been argued that this view is inadequate in its assumption that Christians can function apart from the political order. Christian citizens, it is emphasized, are themselves part of the political order. Modern critics have also argued that this view interprets biblical teaching too much in terms of sixteenth-century political realities. There is some truth to this statement. The Anabaptists' highly negative view of the state probably owes at least as much to the forms of the state that existed in the sixteenth century as to biblical teaching.

Some modern critics have also stated that the emphasis on

being a separate people, almost a separate society, has led to both ethnic segregation and an ethnocentric ethic. Whatever merit the latter criticism may have had in the sixteenth century, it would have less validity today, given the tremendous service ministries, through Mennonite Central Committee, Mennonite Disaster Service, and many other Anabaptist/Mennonite agencies, that heirs of Anabaptism have undertaken in their home communities and around the world.

In our own day we need to say that, like all the other late medieval interpretations of church-state relations, the early Anabaptist view could not have anticipated the profound changes that a state can experience when democratic transformation of the political system occurs. In assessing the classical Anabaptist views, me must keep that reality in mind.

Conclusion

In modern times Anabaptist views of church-state relations, while still generally identified with the theological emphases set forth in the sixteenth century, have been modified. Some observers would say they have been widely compromised by many Anabaptist groups and individuals, both in theory and in practice. Whether all the adaptation and compromise is unfortunate is debatable. Perspectives and evaluations vary greatly.

In recent generations, and especially in recent decades, we see many Mennonites active in politics and government and observe extensive cooperation between Mennonite churches and government.[6] Supporters of such cooperation argue that it is being undertaken to advance the common good, that it is a form of loving one's neighbor. Many modern Mennonites understand the political realm to be like any other sector of a fallen society. It can be an opportunity for service but, as is required in all kinds of involvement in the larger society, Christian participation in politics, whether in elective or other roles, is justifiable only to the extent that Christian discipleship permits.

The heirs of this noble tradition face the challenge of retaining that which is truly biblical, of making modifications where they are warranted, and of applying the central teachings to modern times and to particular church-state situations. In doing so they can be encouraged by the statement by Thomas Sanders with which this chapter began. The Mennonites, particularly the early Anabaptists, "more accurately reproduce the views of the New Testament church than any of the other perspectives toward the state under consideration here." Can it also be said that Mennonites by and large still live by those New Testament views?

4

What Does God Require of Governments?

CONCERNING POLITICAL MATTERS, as in many other areas of life, Jesus did not give his followers detailed instructions. He did, however, leave us the ethics spelled out in the Sermon on the Mount (Matthew 5–7), in the two great commandments (Luke 10:25-37), and in his many lessons and parables. Many of his assertions and guidelines have political relevance.

The various biblical writers have addressed this topic extensively. Throughout the Old Testament we read that God is pleased with rulers who are just, honest, diligent, and God-fearing. Of course, we also read about many rulers who are unjust, dishonest, negligent, and who dishonor God. In fact, in the Old Testament alone there are about one hundred references to unjust rulers who displease God. For example, in Isaiah 59:15 we read that "the LORD looked and was displeased that there was no justice." A more detailed assessment is found in Isaiah 10:1-2: "Woe to those who make unjust laws, to those who issue oppressive decrees, to deprive the poor of their rights, and rob my oppressed people of justice, making widows their prey and robbing the fatherless."

Perhaps the most significant New Testament description of God's requirements for governments is found in Romans 13:1-7:

> Everyone must submit himself to the governing authorities, for there is no authority except that which God has established. The authorities that exist have been established by God. Consequently, he who rebels against the authority is rebelling against what God has instituted, and those who do so will bring judgment on themselves. For rulers hold no terror for those who do right, but for those who do wrong. Do you want to be free from fear of the one in authority? Then do what is right and he will commend you. For he is God's servant to do you good. But if you do wrong, be afraid, for he does not bear the sword for nothing. He is God's servant, an agent of wrath to bring punishment on the wrongdoer. Therefore, it is necessary to submit to the authorities, not only because of possible punishment but also because of conscience. That is also why you pay taxes, for the authorities are God's servants, who give their full time to governing. Give everyone what you owe him: If you owe taxes, pay taxes; if revenue, then revenue; if respect, then respect; if honor, then honor.

In applying the various biblical teachings and exhortations to our time and in utilizing our God-given conscience and common sense, I believe we can identify at least twenty God-pleasing tasks or duties of governments. I suggest further that all twenty have validity for all times and for governments around the globe. Therefore, these can be seen as God's major requirements of governments, particularly but not exclusively regarding national governments.

1. A government has the God-given responsibility to rule. While we might assume that this idea is self-evident, we do well to spell out what we mean, because sometimes governments fail to rule. They simply do not do what is expected of them or even what is logically required of them. Ruling includes leading, assisting, educating, informing, protecting, managing crises, planning, regulating, licensing, persuading, and providing essential services or ensuring that they are provided by others. If governments are unwilling to rule, then they will invite disobedience, defiance, insurrection, and perhaps even anarchy. They will also be responsible for the resulting problems. And, of course, they are displeasing God.

2. **A government should uphold the general good.** Governments constantly face the temptation to cater to special-interest groups, particularly those that helped them become the government, by election, by military conquest, or by some other means. But God expects governments to govern for the public good. They may not govern in a way that benefits only some people, typically a minority, while grossly neglecting or exploiting the rest of the population. That is clearly the intent of Romans 13:1-8.

3. **A government should see its role as a trust.** Governmental officials are merely the officeholders. They have responsibility and power for a limited period of time. The office of government is bigger than they are. It continues indefinitely; their time in office does not! Whether elected or not, they serve only for a time as custodians and stewards of the powers of government. We could also call them trustees, for they have been given a trust. God wants governments to use their time in office to govern well and then to pass the trust on to their successors. As a series of governments see their time in office as a trust and act accordingly, a tradition of decency, moderation, stability, and peaceful transition of governments will, hopefully, develop.

4. People in government are required by God to practice integrity and honesty. Whether involving private relationships, business transactions, or governmental activity, God's standards of personal integrity and honesty are constant. Given the large amounts of other people's money that government officials collect and administer, the temptations for abuse are great. We all know of instances of gross dishonesty by some governmental officials. If government leaders lack integrity and honesty, all their promises and policies are of little consequence. In fact, politicians without integrity are very dangerous people. At their worst they can be office-holding robbers siphoning public money into their personal bank accounts. God will surely judge such leaders very harshly.

5. A government should work hard to establish and maintain a free society. Within reasonable limits a government should nurture and maintain basic freedoms and apply them fairly to all people. These include freedom of assembly, freedom of speech, freedom of association, freedom to travel, freedom of religion, freedom of the press, and political freedom. It may be difficult to extend freedom to those with whom we disagree sharply or those whose beliefs we think are wrong, but in a free society such freedoms ought to be enjoyed by all, provided that people abide by the operating rules of a free society. Thus the right to be in error, as the majority might assess beliefs, must be protected within broad limits even by governments of opposing faiths. A fundamental reason Christians, both as citizens and as government officials, are especially committed to uphold freedom is that God treats us that way. Beginning in the garden of Eden, the all-powerful and eternal God has given his human creatures the right to choose either right or wrong.

6. **A government should respect, promote, and nurture human dignity.** While this guideline applies to all governments, it has special significance for Christians in the political arena because they realize, perhaps more than others, that all people are made in the image of God and possess an eternal soul. They know that God deems a single person to be more valuable than the entire physical world! This fundamental reality causes Christians, perhaps more than most other people, to emphasize the importance of each person in society.

From the Christian viewpoint, people are not the most advanced evolutionary animals; they are creatures made by a creator. Each life has value, each life has dignity, each life has potential, each life has meaning. A government should therefore adopt policies that enhance and protect human dignity. Among other things this means that its hospitals, homes for the aged, prisons, and housing for the destitute must be respectable and not dehumanizing.

7. **A good government has a social conscience and embraces a good measure of humanitarianism.** This means that as funds permit, a good government addresses human needs. It does not stand idly by as certain segments of the population suffer but does what it can to alleviate suffering. If flood, famine, fire, or disease create havoc, such a government will provide relief as it is able to do so. In that sense, a good government reflects the biblical ethic of being "my brother's keeper." Such a government also does what it can to help the elderly, the disabled, orphans, the sick, and any others who are destitute. A good government is like a good neighbor; within the limits of its resources it responds to human need.

The Bible has much to say about the treatment of the most needy in our midst. Society as a whole, in part acting through governments, has a responsibility to come to the aid of those who simply cannot help themselves and have no one else to help them. Decent treatment of the destitute is a particular Christian virtue but also a mark of moral people who are not Christians. It is not right for a government to adopt policies that make the rich richer and the poor poorer. It is wrong for a government to ignore urgent needs or even let the needs become greater!

8. **A government should pay particular attention in its policies to the exploited and the marginalized.** In any society, there are groups of people who seem to be more or less permanently at the bottom of the social and economic ladders. Often they have been exploited and mistreated. Sometimes these people belong to a minority race or a minority religious group. In some societies they are suppressed and exploited because they belong to a lower caste. Governments should not practice or tolerate such systemic discrimination against fellow human beings who are also made in the image of God. Romans 13:4 reminds us that government "is God's servant to do you good." The quality of a government is perhaps best judged by how it treats those at the bottom of the social and economic ladders and how it treats those in prison.

9. **A government is required by God to establish and maintain law and order, to the best of its ability.** Romans 13 and other biblical passages state clearly that a government "is an agent of wrath to bring punishment on the wrong-doer" (verse 4). Evil must be restrained. Individuals must not be allowed to take the law into their own hands, they must not be permitted to run amok with knives, guns, or grenades or to drive vehicles while intoxicated. Crime must be challenged and preferably prevented by both preventive policies and punitive responses. Anarchy must also be prevented.

In the early years of the Christian church, there was a

debate about whether Christians should obey sub-Christian governments. Paul states emphatically that the institution of government, even of a non-Christian government, must be respected and obeyed unless its requirements contradict God's law. In this connection we should point out that it is appropriate for citizens to try to replace the officials entrusted with the power of government, but responsible citizens, including Christians, must not challenge or undermine the underlying institution of government itself.

10. **An inherent function of government is to regulate the exercising of power by other institutions and organizations.** In any society some agency must be the ultimate referee, the final arbiter, the overarching power center. In a stable society the government functions in that capacity. That is what Paul meant when he stated in Romans 13 that the government "does not bear the sword for nothing" (verse 4). Government has the final human word. Within broad bounds it sets the limits of power for labor unions, corporations, ethnic and racial groups, families and tribes, religious communities, and all other groups and organizations. Of course, it also does so for individuals. In striving to create a peaceful and congenial society, good governments seek to persuade as much as possible, to educate, to entice, and to cajole. But in the final analysis, if such undertakings fail, they have received from God the mandate to use coercive power if that is needed.

11. **A good government is committed to the pursuit of justice.** The clamor for justice is universal. It is also timeless. We have already noted that calls for justice abound in both the Old Testament and the New Testament. To achieve justice, government policies must be fair, clear and rea-

sonable. The courts must also be fair. The punishment should always be appropriate to the offense. There is no place for torture, and prisons should be decent and respectable; after all, even the worst offenders are people made in the image of God. They are also people for whom Jesus died. Their sins have also been paid for by our Savior. Through its government, however, society may still pronounce punishment for the breaking of laws. In a good political system much emphasis is also placed on victim-offender reconciliation and on prisoner rehabilitation.

In the pursuit of justice, it is also required that lawmakers and all other government officials must themselves be subject to the laws they make. There is one law for all. There should be no exemptions or special privileges for those who happen, for the present, to be entrusted with the reins and powers of government.

12. **A government should practice procedural fairness.** This means that government departments, courts, and the various regulatory and administrative agencies must be fair in making decisions and distributing benefits. There is no place for arbitrariness or for bribes. Rulings announced by the many agencies of government should be consistent and in general terms predictable. In making decisions, the same policies and rules should be followed for all racial, ethnic, and religious groups. In this connection we should emphasize that government should never use its coercive capability to achieve the goals of one religion or to suppress a religion.

13. **A government should practice fiscal integrity.** There must be honesty and fairness in the collection of taxes and fees, and in the allocation and distribution of government funds. While there may be reasonable differences of opinion concerning whether a government should, for example, raise

taxes or lower taxes, or reduce or expand social programs, there is no difference of opinion concerning the belief that there should be no unnecessary taxation, no unwarranted deficits, no graft, and no corruption. As recorded in Luke 3:12-14, John the Baptist instructed tax collectors to be fair and not to "collect any more than you are required to." That is still good advice today.

14. **A government should implement fair trading laws.** In general, companies and individuals should, within very broad limits, be free to sell and to buy where and when they wish to do so. This same freedom is also a good policy in international trade. However, some governments, especially in the West, have been very hypocritical in this area. Many of them have urged developing countries to expand their economies as rapidly as they can. People in poor countries are often urged to grow crops and to industrialize but then many of these same western countries create huge tariff barriers or grant massive subsidies to their own producers, or introduce restrictive quotas that make it almost impossible for the developing countries to sell their products or resource materials to the major consuming countries. Tariff barriers and other hurdles intended to make others poorer so that those who are already rich can be made richer are as displeasing to God as are falsified scales. Some governments have also taken advantage of their dominance in one sector of trade to extract unjustifiably high prices from those who need what they have to offer. In all these matters, the Christian challenge is to be fair and reasonable and to urge governments to follow such ethical norms.

15. **A government should strive for peace.** While all governments in this fallen, sub-Christian world possess coercive capacity in military and police forms, God's requirement

is that all authorities seek peace as much as possible. The biblical call for peace, even as it concerns governments, is a strong thread from Genesis to Revelation. To be sure, in a few situations God has used specific governments to punish other governments and peoples, but the call, especially in the New Testament, to work for peace is the overarching one. It is noteworthy, in this regard, that although God himself instructed David to undertake some battles against foreign governments and peoples (see 1 Samuel 23:2), he then announced that because David had shed blood, he could not build the temple (see 1 Chronicles 22:6-10).

16. **A government should promote public morality.** Here we encounter a very challenging situation. While it pleases God when governments uphold and promote what is right and moral, governments should not use the arm of the law to try to force people to be Christian or even to behave in a Christian manner. As Jesus explained, the kingdom of God is not built by force, only by human choice. This means that government policies that, for example, oppose abortion as a means of birth control, reject slavery, require a day of rest each week, and punish rape, arson, or theft do so not specifically because the Bible teaches that such behavior is wrong, although that reality may carry considerable weight, but because such behavior is detrimental to society. In such areas the requirements of an enlightened society and Christian ethics overlap.

17. **A good government realizes that it has responsibility for its physical environment.** Governments have a responsibility to prevent the destruction of the environment. The natural world was created by God (see Genesis 1-3; Colossians 1:16). God made land and water, trees and clean air, for us to use, not for us to abuse. He put

human beings in charge to look after his creation. Government itself must model right action. People and corporate agencies that cause God's creation to be polluted and destroyed, who poison water and air and fish and plants, must be brought to heel.

18. **A good government is ready to listen to its critics.** In many democracies those political parties that have lost elections are nonetheless given a special role in the legislature to serve as critics of governments. They serve as a check to keep the government in line, to try to keep it honest and fair, and to be available as an alternate government. Such systems usually work well. Since no government in a political system can function fully according to Christian principles, given that they all function in a fallen world, the population is well served by such institutional checks. Journalists, editors, educators, pressure groups and others can make a very important contribution with their critical comments and their suggestions. Because of their social conscience and their ethics, Christians can be exceptionally effective in this area. A good government does not suppress those who express criticisms and suggestions. Rather, it listens carefully and makes changes and corrections as these are warranted.

19. **All governments should acknowledge that they are servants of God.** Many passages of Scripture make this point. For example, Romans 13 tells us unequivocally that a government is "God's servant" and that "the authorities are God's servants." From the time when governments first appeared to the time when God helped the children of Israel choose their first king, to our own time, all governments actually in office have been servants of God. This is true even when governments deny it or ignore it or are not even aware of it. Time and again our God is called "King of kings and

Lord of lords" (see Revelation 17:14; 19:16). Governments are well advised to acknowledge that reality.

20. All governments should acknowledge that they are accountable to God. It is one thing for a government to acknowledge that it is a servant of God, it is something even more significant for a government to acknowledge that it is ultimately accountable not only to the population of a country but also specifically to God. Governments are accountable to God for the policies they make and for how they implement those policies, for how they rule over the land and its people. God, not they, will have the last word.

At this point some readers may state that because Jesus has left his followers only one ethic, how can we speak of an ethical system for governments that operate at a sub-Christian level? The answer is two-fold. First, and most important, the Bible actually does spell out an amazing number of behavioral guidelines for governments. We must note them and take them seriously. Second, godly people do have advice for those who do not accept God's ethics. We have ethical concerns to express to all people, be they Christians or non-Christians. We can pressure drunks not to drive. We can urge cheaters to stop cheating. We can insist that husbands stop beating their wives. We can try to stop people from torturing animals. We can insist that labels on packaging not state something untrue. And we should try to prevent people from building houses and bridges that will collapse. Similarly, we have ethical concerns, based on Scripture, to relay to governments, however uncommitted the officeholders may be to Christian values.

Sometimes the ethics question is asked in a different form. Are non-Christians in government and non-Christian or even anti-Christian governments also accountable to God?

The Bible makes it clear that they are. Perhaps the most important example involves Belshazzar, king of Babylon in the days of Daniel. After this ungodly ruler had behaved very badly, God told him, "You have been weighed in the scales and found wanting. . . . Your kingdom is divided and given to the Medes and Persians" (Daniel 5:26-27). The Bible is emphatic on this point. All governments and all rulers are accountable to God. In the final analysis God—not the citizenry or any foreign government—will be their judge.

From time to time all governments need to be reminded of this fact. Perhaps, as governments contemplate their awesome task and understand that they are accountable to God, they will take their role very seriously and act more conscientiously. To that end the Christians in government and Christians in society generally can make an important contribution as they draw attention to God's teachings and God's requirements of governments.

5

Can Civil Governments Function According to Christian Ethics?

FOR CENTURIES CHRISTIANS have debated whether governments can function according to the biblical ethics laid out for committed Christians. As I see the matter, the answer is clear. Christian discipleship is the norm for Christians, and though Christian ethics are prescribed for Christians, they are not presented in the Bible as the fundamental norms for the state.

That does not mean, however, that Christian ethics are irrelevant for rulers. They are relevant in two ways. First, every non-Christian is invited, indeed urged, to become a Christian and live by the new ethic. In some situations such a decision may mean a withdrawal from political offices; in many situations it would not require withdrawal. Second, given the broad utility of Christian ethics for non-Christians individually as well as for sub-Christian societies, Christian citizens constantly urge non-Christians, including rulers, to accept as much as possible of the Christian ethic in the practicing of their craft. Christian ethics are good for everyone, even if they cannot be definitive norms for the state. Christian citizens would be well advised to remind rulers of Abraham Lincoln's assertion that "nothing can be politically right if it is morally wrong."

Granted, some problems would arise if governments in a fallen society would actually try to govern entirely by Christian ethics. Does a ruler, even if he is a Christian, have the right to sacrifice his country's advantages or its assets when the large majority of its citizens are opposed? Further, would a ruler be acting correctly if he simply "turned the other cheek," so to speak, and did nothing to stop a brutal foreign dictator from attacking, pillaging, and conquering his country? Should invading soldiers simply be allowed to plunder, rape, kill, and destroy? Should government do nothing to try to stop such evil action? Also, would a government in a relatively prosperous country be acting rightly if it decided, against the wishes of the majority population, to give away the bulk of its assets to poor countries and commit itself simply to follow Jesus in a life of faith, trusting him to provide for its needy people in the future?

These questions suggest that it may not be adequate to try to transfer all Christian ethical norms to a government. The political situation is complex and requires much thought. A fallen society, precisely because it is fallen, does not live ethically like the body of Christ does, or at least like it should. All national governments, and perhaps also all provincial and municipal governments, function at an ethical level far below what Jesus expects of his followers. There is much room for improvement. Since that is the case, Christian citizens should not hesitate to urge governments to adopt more enlightened and more ethical policies and practices.

Could it ever happen that a government might actually decide to govern entirely according to the highest Christian ethic of selflessness and perhaps give away its financial reserves, eliminate all means of protection, and leave the country vulnerable to military attack? There is always the possibility, of course, that an individual political ruler or a government might actually try to do so. There is also the remote possibility that such an improbable achievement might evoke so much surprise and admiration that other governments might not take advantage of the situation. As I read political history, such a situation has never occurred. It is also very unlikely ever to occur in the future.

Problems in Developing Ethics for Governments

Given these realities, many attempts have been made to develop ethical guidelines for governments. These efforts have been difficult because of several factors. First, both the state and the church tend to make absolute ethical claims. The state wants citizens to be ready to place the state as the highest good and be ready to die for it. Millions of young men, and in recent years also young women, have done so. In a sub-Christian society fighting for one's country is seen as one of the highest virtues. The Christian church, positing the acceptance of Christ as the highest good, sees matters differently. It also requires Christians to be prepared to lay down their lives, but in this case it is for the truth and for their faith! These absolutist claims conflict.

A second complicating factor is that church and state pursue fundamentally different and at times contradictory values. Where the church emphasizes obedience to Christ, the state requires obedience to its laws. Where the church teaches self-sacrifice for others, the state seeks security for itself and its citizens. Where the church teaches inclusion of all people, the state underscores exclusion of many people. Where the church stresses persuasion, the state relies ultimately on coercion. Finally, where the church stresses the need for love, the state, as its highest achievement, pursues justice. Understandably, the ethical tensions between the two orders are substantial.

The goals of the two realms are also different; they seek different kinds of ethical outcomes. For the church the ideal is perfection. When Jesus delivered his Sermon on the Mount to the large crowds he urged them to "be perfect, therefore, as your heavenly Father is perfect" (Matthew 5:48). That is the Christian ideal. The state, for its part, delivers a different message. Its aim is to contain evil, maintain social tranquility, and achieve economic progress. Moreover, concerning its citizens, its focus is not on character but on external behavior.

Approaches to Ethical Dualism

In trying to develop appropriate sets of ethics for the government, various proposals have been offered and sometimes implemented. Following his edict in AD 383 that Christianity was to be the state religion of the Roman Empire, Theodosius I tried by formal decree to eliminate the tension between the two orders. Granted, the persecution of Christians ended, but the people of the world still kept on living by their sub-Christian ethics. Changing the law did not automatically change their ethics.

Although both Constantine and Theodosius I tried to blend the two sets of ethical values, they could not get around the reality that the state and the church are, in fact, two distinct orders or kingdoms. Very quickly the differences reasserted themselves, differences that could not be eliminated by decree. Jesus, of course, had himself acknowledged this duality of kingdoms when, during his interrogation by Pontius Pilate, he said, "My kingdom is not of this world. If it were, my servants would fight to prevent my arrest by the Jews. But now my kingdom is from another place" (John 18:36). The apostle Paul invoked the same truth when he said that "flesh and blood cannot inherit the kingdom of God" (1 Corinthians 15:50). There are two kingdoms profoundly different in their ethics.

What Constantine and Theodosius I encountered and what Jesus and Paul described is the basic ethical dualism that has characterized state-church tensions since the church first appeared on the scene. We cannot resolve the dilemma by seeking to marginalize one and nurturing only the other. After all, God is the author of both orders. Moreover, in the fallen world in which the church functions, both church and state are needed. But how does the citizen deal with this duality? And how does the state come to terms with it? And how does the faithful church come to terms with it? Several approaches have been prescribed.

Martin Luther, the great Protestant reformer, acknowledged the existence of the duality. His solution was to have the two ethical systems function within one person, at least if that person is a Christian. Thus, for example, as a Christian a person is guided by the ethic of love and will never kill or undertake violence against another person. But as a magistrate the same person can with a clear conscience authorize violence against a person and order him to be killed. If Christian soldiers embrace such an ethic, it follows that armies of Christians can attack and kill one another and no one is guilty of any wrongdoing. According to this reasoning, it is not the people as Christians who were doing the killing; it is the people as soldiers. The Christian soldiers and their supporters thus see themselves as innocent.

Having two sets of ethics in operation within one person produces major problems. Is it always clear in which role one is functioning? Can a person truly be fully committed to two opposing sets of ethics? Can he do so without experiencing serious self-doubt or even mental anguish? Would acceptance of such dualism not lead to rationalization of much that would otherwise be seen as morally wrong? More importantly, does God accept such a division of ethical standards within one person? Additional criticisms of Luther's doctrine of dual ethics within one person are that his emphasis on civic submission tends to produce nationalistic Christianity. It tends to promote civic passivity, a passivity that in the twentieth century, for example, made it easier for Adolf Hitler to implement his brutal Nazi policies.

The sixteenth-century Anabaptist reformers formulated a third understanding of how the two ethical systems can operate in a country. Conrad Grebel, Menno Simons, and others argued that each of the two ethical systems should be associated with a specific community. Thus the church would be an ethical community unto itself, and the fallen world, even with Christians in its midst, would follow a lower ethic and would also be an ethical community unto itself. The Christian community would be committed to the high Christian ethic. The fallen world would follow a lower ethic. An important biblical text invoked to support this stance is 2 Corinthians 6:17: "Therefore come out from them and be separate, says the Lord."

While this approach ranks high on consistency and integrity, it did not sit well with the governments at the time or with most later governments. Rulers, as well as other Christians, accused proponents of this view of being unconcerned about the survival, let alone the well-being, of the political regimes or even the survival of the country in which they lived. The Anabaptists/Mennonites responded with the assertion that the state is not the bearer of the meaning of history. God has called the church, not the state, to be his messenger. Christians must therefore be faithful to and primarily concerned about the church, not the state. They argued that the survival of a state, any political state, is not a priority for the Christian church. It has a different agenda.

A significant shortcoming of the classical Anabaptist view is that the two communities cannot generally be separated geographically. They cannot function as separate political communities. Sometimes this attempted separation of ethical communities was accompanied by social and geographical separation, as with the Hutterite communes. Sometimes it was accompanied by geographical distancing from a society becoming too invasive, as when thousands of very conservative Mennonites left Canada in the 1920s to move en masse to Mexico. And sometimes it was accompanied by emigration to a new land where major exemptions would be granted, as when Mennonites migrated en masse from Prussia and Poland to imperial Russia in the late eighteenth and early nineteenth centuries. Then, when these exemptions and privileges were partially lost after 1862, thousands migrated to the United States and Canada and sought similar exemptions in their new homelands.

The question of how the two communities or kingdoms ought to relate to one another, how they can both function successfully in the same territory, has not been adequately answered. If Anabaptists try to live in their own territory, in doing so they immediately create a political regime that tends to become similar to the one they are trying to avoid. The Mennonite experience in Russia came very close to creating such a situation. Maybe there is no final solution to this Anabaptist/Mennonite dilemma. Maybe such Christian citizens and the secular governments under which they live must simply learn to live with serious tensions and try as best they can to reach compromise solutions for specific problems as they arise. Where compromise is not acceptable to the Christians, they must accept the difficult consequences: either departure for some other jurisdiction or acceptance of harassment and punishment, in some cases even to the point of dying for their beliefs.

A fourth response, less well known, is gaining ground in some western countries. Here the argument holds that Christians in politics are not responsible for carrying out anti-Christian policies and practices if they do so because a majority of their constituents has asked them to do so. This view is sometimes called populism. If the people want something done that is not good and you do it only because of your constituency's wishes, then you are excused, so the argument goes, and you are not guilty of violating the Christian ethic. You are only an agent, not the responsible actor. You are absolved of wrongdoing. I find no biblical basis for such a view.

This argument, flawed as it is, is not new. Its basic argument was adopted by Aaron when he sculptured a golden idol in the form of a calf because the Israelites pressured him to do so (see Exodus 32.) He was, he argued, not personally guilty; after all, he was only doing what the people wanted him to do. For true believers of any faith in any age, such rationalization is not acceptable.

A fifth approach might be termed utopian theocracy. The central assumption here is that the dilemma of ethical dualism can be resolved, at least for some Christians and some political rulers, by the establishment of a political community, whether municipal, provincial, or national, in which civil government implements a Christian ethic or at least makes that its goal. The hope is that the ethical tensions between church and government will be erased. Many such experiments involving small communities have been attempted in the British Isles, continental Europe, the United States, Canada, and elsewhere. John Calvin's Geneva could be described as such an experiment. All of these efforts have failed. Even when a political experiment begins with only fully committed Christians, fallen humanity rather quickly deteriorates to the point where persuasion fails and coercion must be employed to maintain law and order.

A sixth approach in coming to terms with the two differing ethical regimes is a modification of the classical Anabaptist view. The approach that I have termed Reformed Anabaptism still holds to the notion of the two separate communities, the church and the rest of society, but it envisions a relationship between the two that is different from the one the early Anabaptists described.

Reformed Anabaptism

Reformed Anabaptism does not assume any social isolation or geographical removal of the Christian community from the mainstream of society. Christians function as a spiritual community. But Christians also function in and as a part of society, impacting it as the salt of the earth. They should be committed to increasing civic righteousness in the public square, which is God's secondary institutional expression of divine compassion. In this view, there is much room for active involvement by Christian citizens in the political order.

What would be the limits of such involvement? Political involvement would be appropriate up to the point that it does not violate Christ's ethic. Therefore, depending on the ethical level of the host country or society, such involvement could be minimal or very extensive. In harsh dictatorships, the involvement by Reformed Anabaptists would likely be very minimal. Perhaps it would not even be permitted. In mature democracies, on the other hand, where government and church have significant overlapping agendas, it could be very extensive. In this approach, the church can support good government policies. And many values taught by the church could be implemented or at least supported by the government. Education, safety, healthcare, and care for the elderly are obvious examples.

The early Anabaptists would have been puzzled by such reasoning. And that is hardly surprising, given that they experienced the state as negative, intolerant, oppressive, and often very brutal.

In recent decades, many contemporary Mennonites have moved toward this understanding. Interestingly, increasing numbers of Christians from other faith communities are also accepting this option. Selective involvement, while holding to one Christian ethic, carries great potential.

It must be acknowledged concerning this perspective that if governments become truly intolerant and oppressive, people holding this view must ultimately accept the same options as did the classical Anabaptists, namely, living with unsatisfactory compromises, fleeing to other places, or accepting persecution.

We thus have six ways of trying to deal politically with the fact that civil governments cannot function according to Christian ethics. Constantine and Theodosius I attempted organizational and operational fusion of the two ethics. Martin Luther and John Calvin placed dualism in the individual believer, whether ruler or citizen. Conrad Grebel and Menno Simons offered dualism in separate communities. Advocates of political populism have offered a peculiar dualism in which a functional dualism is present within lawmakers and rulers, but it is not actually part of their personal ethical system. Utopian theocracy attempts to transform society into the church. Reformed Anabaptism accepts dualism in communities but proposes penetration of society by Christians to the extent that adherence to Jesus' ethic permits.

While these are the basic options, mostly rooted in history, in our day we find variations of all of them in the modern world. It is not possible to describe these in detail here. We must acknowledge that they exist and that these various approaches are still evolving. For me it is especially significant that the basic ethical content of the Lutheran approach has changed very little and remains the one dominant among Christians to this day. Most Christians throughout the world accept this dualism within the individual believer.

Promoting a Christian Ethic

This brings us to another key question. Even though civil government cannot, generally speaking, function according to the Christian ethic, should it nevertheless promote a particular ethic, specifically the Christian or Judeo-Christian ethic? My assessment is that to a large extent it should do so. And the basic reason is that it is in everyone's interest if the government does so.

My argument is as follows. Of all the major ethical systems in the world, the Christian ethic, which can also be called the Judeo-Christian ethic, is easily the most useful—

and I use the term advisedly—in helping governments to achieve a free, democratic, tolerant, and respectful society in which human dignity is affirmed and serious social needs are addressed.

Of all the world's major religions, Christianity is far and away the strongest in advocating choice and voluntarism. It does so because that is how God treats human beings. From creation on, God has given human beings choice and respected their decisions, faulty though they may be. Although Christians have often not fully practiced the Christian ethic of tolerance and love, the basic emphases and their societal utility have not changed. It is thus no mere coincidence that the countries in the world where freedom is most firmly rooted, where rights are most strongly respected, are almost all part of Christendom, that part of the world where Christianity is the dominant faith. It is therefore hardly surprising that the great philosopher and theologian Reinhold Niebuhr once observed, "Democracy is that child of which Christianity need never be ashamed."

Because the Christian ethic is conducive to freedom, toleration, and respect for dissenters, adherents of other faiths have often supported the nurturing of Christian values. They know well in which countries religious dissenters are tolerated and respected. They know that in many, perhaps most, countries of the world where other religions are dominant, such freedoms and respect do not exist.

While the above statements are true, they are not the whole truth. Without a doubt Christianity is conducive to freedom but, unfortunately, throughout history some governments, while proclaiming their commitment to Christianity, have denied basic freedoms. The Spanish Inquisition, the denial of basic freedoms in Cromwellian England, and oppression in the Puritan colonies in America come to mind. What is the explanation? It is that these political authorities did not actually practice basic Christian principles. They claimed that they were doing so, but they actually were doing the opposite.

At this point I want to emphasize that a significant Christian ethos, or a partial Christian ethic, can exist in a country even though the actual practice of Christianity is only shallow or spotty. Over time the lingering Christian ethical values will weaken if the actual practice of Christianity declines. But their resilience, as demonstrated in our own day in numerous countries in Western Europe and North America, is quite remarkable.

It is sad that in our day many governments, including many in countries with a strong Christian heritage, apparently do not realize that it is in their own interest, as rulers trying to control evil and to reward what is good, to cultivate a vigorous Christian ethos in the private sector. The Christian ethic, with its respect for others, its rejection of fatalism, its emphasis on choice, its fear of divine punishment in eternity, its emphasis on love and deeds of kindness, and its personal accountability to civil government and ultimately to God, is probably the best soil in which good citizenship thrives.

Conclusion

This brief survey has shown that because of the fundamental differences between the ethical system inherent in the political order and the Christlike, servant ethical system inherent in the faithful Christian church, civil governments cannot function according to the Christian ethic. An exception might be possible in the most improbable situation in which virtually all citizens in some political jurisdiction are transformed believers. No such situation has ever flourished. The discipleship ethic, quite logically, is found in the community of Christian disciples, not in the political order.

In conclusion I must emphasize that the ethical dualism we have analyzed was not created by God. It is the result of moral choices made by human beings to whom God gave moral freedom. Faulty human choice, not divine direction, made necessary the establishment of the political order which, in turn, has created the moral dilemma Christian citizens encounter.

Which of the options surveyed is best? While no human being can claim to comprehend all the potential and all the consequences of each one of them, for me the evidence is compelling. On the basis of my understanding of New Testament Scripture and of the political order, it seems to me that Reformed Anabaptism is the best option. It is best for Christians because it combines faithfulness to the Christian ethic with effective Christian servanthood. To the extent that Christian ethics can be practiced by governments it is best for governments because it prescribes ethical values that benefit everybody, and it sets out a way in which enlightened rulers can utilize the idealism and commitment of faithful Christians in advancing the cause of civic righteousness.

6

What Does God Require of Christian Citizens?

THE MAIN THESIS of this chapter is that God has a role for Christians in the political realm and that we ought to give serious consideration to carrying out that role faithfully. Such an understanding has not been supported by all Christians in the past nor is it supported by all Christians now. There have been voices urging avoidance. For example, in AD 215 the early Christian theologian Tertullian wrote, "Nothing is more foreign to us Christians than politics." At a time when ordinary citizens had virtually no rights and very little opportunity to influence decision makers, such a view may have seemed appropriate; it strikes me, however, as being inadequate and biblically unwarranted. I suggest that it is doubly unwarranted if we are privileged to live in democratic, free societies.

Why should individual Christians view the political order as an arena of opportunity, influence, and responsibility? Why not simply let the sub-Christian society tend to its own structures and problems while we Christians concentrate solely on the biblical mandate to evangelize the world and teach people to follow Jesus? As I understand the Scriptures and as I look at our situation in society, it seems to me that there are major reasons why Christians should give careful thought to political matters.

1. The political order is a parallel, although secondary, order functioning alongside the church to serve God's human creation. Government, as the agency of the state, is the expression of God's love and especially of his providence toward those people who reject his lordship as experienced in the Christian church and proclaimed by it.

2. God can achieve considerable good through the operation of the political order, namely, the prevention of anarchy, the restraint of evil, the maintenance of law and order, as well as the maintenance of conditions that, generally speaking, facilitate the carrying out of the great commission.

3. Church and state share many concerns and goals. This reality is hardly surprising given that many of the positive services that the state now undertakes were first pioneered by the church. Indeed, many are still carried on by the faithful church.

4. Although we may not realize it, most of us are much more involved in the political realm than we know. The political realm has become a substantial part of our social environment. Detachment and irrelevance are no longer options; perhaps they never were.

5. Government is big and growing. Its tentacles now impact the church and the life of individual Christians in massive ways. Although there are many positive aspects to this expansion of political power and regulation, there are also many negative effects. Further, in most countries the government now makes claims and demands that specifically contradict how Christians ought to live. In many

western countries, for example, including Canada and parts of the United States, such demands include the approval of same-sex marriages and other practices that both church and state previously rejected. These initiatives need to be challenged and addressed.

6. No part of a Christian's life lies outside the scope of Christ's lordship. Christ is also Lord of the political order. Understanding exactly what this means is an ongoing challenge for every Christian.

7. We may not be "of the world" (John 15:19), but we are certainly in the world. God, in his wisdom, has chosen us to be his representatives, his messengers, here on earth. Since that is the case, should we not become knowledgeable about the social setting into which God has placed us? Show me someone who loudly proclaims his overarching concern for "the lost" but who is oblivious to what is happening in the world, including the political world, and I'll show you someone without much credibility. In the political realm, as in human relations generally, where there is real interest there will also be a desire to become knowledgeable about the object of one's interest. In fact, given that God loves the world even in its fallen state (see John 3:16), should those who worship God and seek to be faithful to his ethical values not also love that same world? And love, we know, always evokes a desire to get to know the object of one's love.

What, then, in specific terms, does God require of Christian citizens in a world permeated by politics? As I see it, there are at least ten specific requirements.

1. **We are to affirm the legitimacy of the state and its government and to submit to it.** First Peter 2:13-15 instructs us to show honor and respect. We are to do this "for the Lord's

sake" to counteract "the ignorant talk of foolish men" who may assert that Christians are anti-government and inclined toward anarchy. While Christians, at times, may have good reason to oppose certain government policies and actions, may work for the removal of some politicians, and may even support the replacement of one political system or ideology with another, we may never reject the necessity and propriety of the institution of government. Faithful Christians do not support or endorse anarchy.

2. **We are to be law-abiding citizens.** Christian citizens should be known as honest, trustworthy, dependable, and law-abiding people. Even when we strive to have laws and policies changed, we try to obey the law as much as we can. There are, of course, exceptions. When political authorities overstep their bounds, when they try to hinder us from being obedient to God, which is our over-riding commitment, then, like the apostles in the first century, we must disobey our rulers (see Acts 4:13-21; 5:23-29.) When this happens, we peacefully accept the consequences, the way Martin Luther King Jr. and countless others have done.

3. **We are to be informed.** In Matthew 16:3 Jesus is quoted as rebuking the Pharisees because they could not "read the signs of the times." Clearly Jesus thought that being informed about what is happening in our society is important. In political matters, as in other dimensions of life, we ought to make an effort to "read the signs of the times." God wants us to be interested in all his agencies on earth.

We all encounter Christians who believe that they have no obligation to find out what is going on in their community or the world. Such an attitude puzzles me. How can we come to grips with Jesus' instruction to be good to our neighbors if we remain ignorant about them and if we do not care what is being done to or by them?

4. **We ought to be the government's most perceptive and useful critics.** This guideline requires considerable explanation. Precisely because we hold to Christ's higher ethic, we have a basis, a measuring rod if you will, for assessing and addressing all sub-Christian performance, including our own. Accordingly, even as we obey a law we do not like, or as we disobey a law that would require us to act in a God-displeasing manner, we urge our rulers to improve their policies. The issue at hand may involve racism, prejudice in immigration regulations, corruption in the bureaucracy or among elected lawmakers, the abuse of foreign aid, militarism, desecration of the environment, procedural or judicial injustice, and much more.

As we seek to be responsible Christian critics, we should realize that governments will likely not be favorably impressed if the only issues about which we protest are those which are self-serving, which benefit us specifically. If we advance only our own causes and ignore the pressing needs of others, what are we doing more than self-centered groups do? If we advance only our own interests, our credibility will likely be very low. All other groups do the same; they also look after their own interests. If we Christians do nothing more, how are we different?

In keeping with the biblical imperative that calls all people and institutions to live by godly principles of justice, righteousness, truth, humanitarianism, the promotion of human dignity, and the pursuit of peace, we courageously remind all peoples and all governments that God's standards have not changed. We remind others of this truth even while we strive to model adherence to God's standards. Christians should never stop moralizing about evil policies and practices. If we address evil, we are following Jesus' example.

An especially difficult problem arises when a country is tempted to think of itself as God's favorite, even as a new

Israel. While it may happen, as in Old Testament times, that God decides to use one country to punish another country for its evil ways, it is inappropriate for any government or country to describe itself as God's agent. Such a selection or decision is strictly God's prerogative. In our day, so-called Christian-Americanism has been a temptation for some American Christians. In earlier times, similar cultic claims gained support in Russia, Great Britain, Spain, Germany, and other lands.[1]

Further, a similar problem exists when the government of any country claims God as a modern-day mascot, patron, or ally, as happens often. In making such claims, rulers ignore the fact that God does not describe himself that way. He is no tribal deity. God clearly and unequivocally describes himself as the King of kings and the Lord of lords who will judge all people and all authorities. He is not the national chaplain of any one country or government.

Similarly, when the government of any country claims that its policies, including its foreign policies, are uniquely righteous, that it is the power of light combating the powers of darkness, as also happens, then Christian critics must speak up. They must remind that particular government that all national governments are less than altruistic, that they all exist to advance their own interests. Moreover they all have some darkness in their own political perspective, public policies, and historical record.

Permit me a personal example of Christian criticism. Some years ago in a published article I strongly criticized the Canadian government for apparently planning to function as a "merchant of death." I used that label because the government was considering how best to help a tobacco marketing board promote the sale of Canadian tobacco in various African countries and other parts of the developing world. I said that the government would be "peddling poison." My article was reported and quoted in major newspapers. Canada's largest newspaper, *The Toronto Star,* included the following statement in its news story: "Redekop said it would be 'un-Christian' and smack of racism for the government to promote tobacco consumption overseas because Canadians would be exploiting an almost non-white Third World."[2]

I don't know how significant my nationally reported opposition was, but I know that soon after the newspapers reported my stance and the growing objection among Christians and many other Canadians, the Canadian government decided not to go ahead with such a plan. The fact that at the time I was moderator of the Canadian Conference of Mennonite Brethren Churches and vice-president of the Evangelical Fellowship of Canada gave additional weight to my objections. If God puts us in positions of potential influence for good, we have a responsibility to use such opportunities to do what is good.

We do not all have equally significant opportunities to express Christian views to rulers. We are not all able to gain media attention, but we can all support those who do have such opportunities, and we can all pray for them as well as for more righteousness in the political realm. Most of us can also write letters, sign petitions, or phone authorities and express our comments to them. For many of us, the whole e-mail system presents a new and easy means to respond quickly.

Let me say one thing more concerning our role as perceptive critics. If we want to be truly effective and taken seriously by government authorities, we should affirm them when we can so that we can with credibility criticize when we must.

5. We should be thankful. We are instructed to be thankful for the institution of government. God has established it for the benefit of all people. The Bible underscores the point (see 1 Timothy 2:1-3). If possible we should also thank God for the rulers of the day. After all, they are the ones who make the whole system work. In situations where the rulers are brutal and evil, it may still be possible to be thankful that the situation is not worse than it is. There may also be specific policies for which we can be thankful.

6. **We should faithfully pay our taxes.** Some Christians do not support such a stance. They argue that Christians, especially those of us who belong to one of the historic peace churches, should withhold that percentage of the taxes that is presumably being used for wrongful causes, particularly to pay for the country's military establishment. I have a thick file of articles justifying this view. Some very godly people hold to such a view. I respect them. They are contributing to a very important debate.

While I largely agree with these people's motivation and goal, I cannot agree with their methods. In the first place, it is almost impossible to ascertain, with even a general degree of accuracy, what part of my tax monies are used for what purposes. Should one also try to calculate what part of one's taxes goes to pay the interest costs and the principal on debts caused partly by earlier wars? Should one include calculations about pensions for veterans and their spouses? As a symbol, tax withholding makes a statement. As a realistic calculation, it strikes me as being problematic.

In the second place, can one seriously argue that a government should have no military capacity when such resources are needed to maintain law and order and to deal with situations of natural catastrophe? In fact, if people say that a government should not have any military might, they are really saying that it should cease being a government. Is that a view which Christians should be championing? By definition a government must have the capacity to enforce its laws. It must have the ability to protect its citizens. That is surely what Paul meant when he said that the government "does not bear the sword for nothing" (Romans 13:4). Quite frankly, to argue that a national government should not have any military capacity, which is the backup for the police forces, comes very close to arguing for anarchy.

In the third place, I find no biblical support for such a stance. Quite to the contrary, Jesus seems to have gone out of his way to model the propriety of paying taxes. Granted, the temple tax was both a religious and a political payment (see Matthew 17:24-26). But Jesus also addressed the payment of regular political taxes. The Herodians asked him one day, "Is it right to pay taxes to Caesar or not?" Jesus' unequivocal response was, "Give to Caesar what is Caesar's and to God what is God's" (Matthew 22:17,21). I do not find much room for serious debate here. The exhortation is clear, and it is particularly telling in that Jesus lived in a colonial setting under an oppressive dictatorship that opposed him and his teaching. In Romans 13:6-7, Paul, despite the brutal treatment many political authorities meted out to him, also strongly endorses the payment of taxes. He makes a significant comment when he writes, "This is also why you pay taxes" (Romans 13:6). Payment of taxes is assumed. The issue is not up for debate.

In sum, I find myself agreeing with the observation of U.S. Supreme Court Justice Oliver Wendell Holmes: "Taxes are the price of civilization." When Jesus taught and practiced the payment of taxes, he was probably concurring with this view.

7. **We should support good policies.** Governments should expect us to support morally sound policies. I think that God also expects that of us. After all, God opposes all that is evil and identifies with all that is good. We should do likewise. A personally written letter, a phone call, or

some other communication can have great effect. Since most citizens are much more inclined to communicate criticism than support, our Christian expressions of support for what is true and right and good will be most welcome and will have effect.

Some years ago I was part of an MCC Canada delegation that had requested time to visit with the Canadian Minister of Indian Affairs in Ottawa. We were given a time to be at his office. When we arrived it became clear that the minister was very busy and had only about fifteen minutes or so to meet with us. He asked what we wanted. We responded that we wanted him and his government to move ahead with their stated intentions of pursuing more enlightened policies toward native people, that we had some specific suggestions, and that we would do what we could to help. He was amazed. He asked if we were asking for any favors or special policies for ourselves. We said no. He then indicated that he had a lot of time for us, and we spent much of the evening with him.

8. **We should pray for our political rulers.** Many biblical passages urge us to pray for rulers. First Timothy 2:1-2 stresses that point. In Psalm 122:6 the people are urged to pray for the peace of Jerusalem. Ezra 6:10 instructs hearers to "pray for the well-being of the king and his sons." Lest we think that such exhortations apply only in settings where we live under wise rulers, Jesus states, "Pray for those who persecute you" (Matthew 5:44) and "pray for those who mistreat you" (Luke 6:28).

9. **We ought to be willing to become involved in the political process.** While I agree that the democratic right to vote in an election includes the right not to vote, I do believe that it pleases God when we use this hardly noticed but still very significant opportunity to influence the selection of rulers

and the shaping of policies. In supporting the existence of a political system that God has established, a further issue is whether we are also willing to become involved more substantively. I firmly believe that if we are willing to do so, the opportunities will arise for at least some of us.

Let us not be too quick to excuse ourselves. As someone once said, "It is much easier to worship Jesus than to obey him." Maybe we need to remind ourselves that faith equals faithfulness and the path to holiness passes through the world of action.

10. **As Christian citizens we ought to remind our rulers that they are accountable to God.** Our rulers need to know that both as individuals and as governments they are ultimately accountable to a sovereign God. They need to hear that some day they will answer to him for how they lived their personal lives as well as for how they used the power and authority he delegated to them. There is a Prime Minister of prime ministers, a King of kings, and a President of presidents who will someday call them to account.

Jesus made the point of God's sovereignty very clear to Pilate when he said, "You would have no power over me if it were not given to you from above" (John 19:11). Pilate apparently did not dispute the point and, judging by his subsequent action, seems to have agreed with Jesus.

Concerning the more personal undertaking of witnessing to rulers about their personal relationship to almighty God, Paul has left us a powerful example. Although a prisoner, and thus of low social standing in that situation, Paul courageously presented the gospel to King Agrippa. His testimony must have been effective because King Agrippa responded by implying that he was almost persuaded to become a Christian. (See Acts 26:25-32.)

The apostle Paul was faithful in presenting Christian truth and Christian claims to the political authorities of his day. He participated in the political realm as he had opportunity. That is also what God requires of us, nothing more and nothing less. Of course, not everyone needs to be equally involved. We have varying abilities and callings. But we should all be knowledgeable and grateful and be willing to do what we can, motivated by our love for God and others, for a fallen world. Let us be faithful in ways that our situations permit and involved to the extent that opportunities arise. Such a commitment and such actions are part of faithful Christian discipleship and obedient Christian servanthood.

7

Christians and Political Involvement: Why? When? How?

THREE GENERAL ASSUMPTIONS should guide us as we deal with this topic. First, being a Christian involves two important matters: accepting the salvation Jesus offers and living a life of obedient discipleship. We must never forget either of them. Nor should we forget that the latter may lead us into arenas of witness and ministry we had not anticipated or even imagined.

Second, Jesus' followers have been called to proclaim that God's lordship extends to all people and to all human organizations and structures. God's compassion spans the earth. Everything belongs to God. "All the world" (Mark 16:15) allows for no exceptions in terms of either geography or people. No people and no social structures escape God's concern or judgment.

Third, in light of the first two assumptions, Christians have an obligation to bring Christian concerns to bear at all levels of human activity, including politics. And let us not be discouraged if we are in a minority, if our numbers are few. As devotional writer Selwyn Hughes observed, "It is the ten righteous people who spare the Sodoms of this world."

Several other personal assumptions need to be stated at the outset. As explained elsewhere, I accept a qualified two-kingdom view of the church and the political order with the church as the preeminent kingdom. Throughout history, God has had "his people," first the children of Israel and then the church of Jesus Christ. But he has also established the political order as a second-best arrangement for those of his human creatures who did not accept his lordship. Christians function in both of these realms but in different ways. Rooted in the kingdom of God, they give primary allegiance and attention to the claims, values, and challenges of the church, but they also take the earthly kingdom seriously. The acceptance of a two-kingdom view also helps us to understand that the political realm should be seen both as an object of Christian ministry and as a channel of Christian service.

Further, I hold to the view, supported by vast historical evidence, that an intrinsically unchristian society, especially if it is democratic, can be improved substantially by good input and enlightened decisions in the political arena. In particular I believe that it can be made more just and more humanitarian by means of Christian influence. Of course, enlightened contributions rooted in other worldviews and religions can also impact a society positively. After all, not all good ideas emanate from the Judeo-Christian worldview. Governments can benefit from humanitarian ideas rooted in other faiths and philosophies. They can enact enlightened laws for a variety of reasons.

It is important to note that there are shades of gray, ethically speaking, among the sub-Christian countries of this world. A British government led by Tony Blair is hardly in the same league as a Korean government led by Kim Il Sung. And the ethical standards of South Africa governed by Nelson Mandela were massively better than those found in Uganda when governed by Idi Amin. Situations within countries are also constantly changing. For example, in the United States and many other western countries, the racial policies of recent decades constitute fundamental progress when compared to the practice of slavery found in those lands in earlier times. And life in contemporary Russia is much better than it was under Joseph Stalin. Similar examples abound.

These realities remind us powerfully that although societies function at a sub-Christian ethical level and although governments enact legislation and conduct their daily affairs in a sub-Christian manner, improvement does happen. While impetus for improvement can come from many sources, Christianity has been a major source of the reforms, such as those achieved by William Wilberforce and Martin Luther King Jr.

Despite the historical evidence, a number of Christians see little value in political action and tend to withdraw from the political realm. That puzzles me, because we know that when godly people withdraw from the political arena, those holding less worthy views will have greater influence. And as the scope and reach of government continue to increase, such withdrawal from the political arena will have ever-increasing consequences. Politically apathetic Christians are well advised to heed the challenge of Carl F. H. Henry when he urged Christians to "roll back the inroads of darkness." Many of these inroads involve government regulation and legislation.

Christian withdrawal and apathy are widely evident. Many Christians never express a word of political commendation or criticism to the authorities nor do they work through any agency to provide citizen input. For decades they don't write a letter. (No postage is required to write MPs in Canada.) Sometimes such people then turn around and strongly criticize politicians and civil servants for lacking any Christian sense of decency. But perhaps these Christians are themselves partly to blame. Have they done their part—have we done our part—to uphold and promote righteousness, justice, decency, and human dignity?

Of course, political involvement can be risky and disappointing, for various reasons. Our understanding either of biblical instruction or of the political problems may be inadequate. Our knowledge of the political system may be faulty. Our methods may be inappropriate. Our expression of Christian concerns may be rejected. And non-Christians or even fellow Christians may misunderstand our motives. Those are some of the risks we must face if we want to be faithful in this area. I am convinced, though, that if we do our best, God will use our efforts for his glory, for improvement in the political realm, and for the building of his kingdom.

In political matters, as in other activity, we must remember that we do not all have the same gifts. We are not all called to do the same tasks. We are not all called or gifted to be heavily involved in political activity. Maybe only a few Christians are called to be active in political arenas. Others may be called to do much less, to be only marginally involved. Some can be encouragers. All can write a letter. Some, perhaps many, may be called to undertake intercessory prayer. As different parts of one body, the church of Jesus Christ, we complement one another and support one another in our various roles.

Several additional ethical truths should influence us in evaluating political activity. We do well to remind ourselves that moral indifference can produce devastating results. If we say that there is no reason to do good or to challenge the evil in our day, we are letting self-centeredness and ignorance blind us to the moral imperative modeled and taught by Jesus. He did not hesitate to challenge evil where he encountered it. Neither should we!

Further, a purely individualistic love for one's neighbor is not enough in our day. Maybe it never was. There are times when faithful Christians need to address societal evil, corporate evil, and the agents of evil. We ought to do so for at least two reasons. First, we are partly responsible, especially in a democracy, for what our governments do; we are citizens and we have opportunities to elect and to influence lawmakers. Second, if we have opportunity to have input and to do good in the political realm but we neglect to do so, we are guilty of the sin of omission against which Scripture strongly warns us (see James 4:17).

Another ethical assertion is that while Christianity has a monopoly on salvation, at least from a Christian perspective, it has no monopoly on compassion. If we consciously acknowledge that fact, we will be better equipped to work alongside non-Christians who share our desire to address problems, help people, and improve conditions in our society, in our country, and abroad.

A very important ethical reminder is this: opportunity plus ability equals accountability. This little equation has often been an excellent reminder to me as I have faced diffi-cult situations that invited my attention or involvement. We can be tempted to ignore some social or political problems and simply go on to other matters, perhaps personal interests or important ministries in the church. We can pass by on the other side, as some religious folk did in the parable of the good Samaritan (see Luke 10:25-37). But if we see a real need and we are in a position to do something positive, God expects us to do so. Christians rightly make much of sins of commission; perhaps it is time that we pay closer attention to sins of omission.

Why Christians Should Be Involved Politically

It has often been said that since Jesus and his disciples did not get involved in the political realm, Christians today should not do so either. Three responses are important. First, Jesus had a unique mission. He concentrated on that divine man-date. We do not have that mission. We are not founders of the Christian church; we are Jesus' followers. Second, in many areas of life, Jesus and his disciples did not actually model behavior for us. For example, Jesus was never a human father or grandfather. He was not a husband or a businessman. He did not model how to become a gracious older Christian. What Jesus did leave us are general ethical values and a mind, guided by the Holy Spirit, to aid us in applying those values in whatever situation we find ourselves. I suggest that, in many areas of life, the challenge is to apply Jesus' teaching more than to follow his earthly example. Our mandate is to be salt and light in a needy world.

Third, it is also the case, of course, that today the political situation in most countries, especially democratic ones, is vastly different from Palestine's in Jesus' day. Palestine in the first century was a colony governed by a harsh dictatorship. The official government was remote, imperial, and unresponsive. Local authorities basically took orders from Rome. There was almost no opportunity for citizen input. Today, in most countries, Christians have considerable opportunity to be heard, to make a difference in the political realm. Greater opportunity creates greater responsibility.

As we contemplate the pros and cons of political involvement, several other realities should be noted. Especially in the western world, government has replaced the church as the most important agency influencing people. That fact makes political awareness and involvement all the more important for Christians today. Many governments now function in a pervasive manner reminiscent of the medieval church before the modern state evolved. Their extensive regulatory, proprietary, and social assistance programs, and their almost total control of the economy influence us every day. In other words, if we want to address what is really important for people today, we cannot ignore the political realm. This holds true even in many developing countries, where governments also seem to be functioning increasingly as a pervasive and domineering reality.

Related to the above preeminence of government activity is the changed nature of much of what most governments do. No longer are they preoccupied only with maintaining roads, strengthening defenses, operating the postal system, and upholding national honor. Most governments now undertake major activity in areas such as health, welfare, insurance, emergency relief, disease control, sanitation, hospital services, placement of orphans, care for the disabled, control of HIV/AIDS, environmental management, childhood education, higher education, professional training, assistance for the poor and the elderly, pension regulation, maintenance of safety, quality standards in production and trade, child labor, and much more.

This changed nature of government in most countries also means that involvement in government, including its many departments and agencies, often presents great opportunities to do good deeds, to assist with tasks that overlap extensively with what Christians do in the private sector. This overlap should not surprise us because Christians pioneered many of these positive governmental activities in the first place!

Even if in a particular country the government does not have the resources to address all these matters, there are typically enough praiseworthy governmental programs to challenge sensitive Christians to become involved. In Jesus' day, there were few, if any, such opportunities in the political realm. In that setting, as in some countries today, doing good deeds means serving in the private sector.

Let us now specifically answer the question, Why should Christians get involved in the political realm, whatever the level of activity might be?

1. We get involved because we want to be responsible citizens. Our common sense tells us that some government policies are better than others. We believe that, together with many other citizens of good will, we can influence governments to choose those that are better. Government

can make society more fair, humanitarian, and civilized. We want to help achieve that end, even though we do not always have explicit biblical directives and cannot always say, "Thus says the Lord."

2. We get involved because we are aware of the biblical guidelines for government (see, for example, Romans 13:1-7 and the appendix). We want to make certain that these guidelines are communicated to government leaders who may not be aware of divine expectations or of divine accountability. We also articulate the biblical guidelines because we want to improve the moral climate in society. We know that the major biblical requirement of government is to curtail evil and reward what is good. Therefore, Christians have a particular responsibility to help governments understand that requirement.

   Concerning the nurturing of a moral climate, one that will benefit all people, we should take to heart this useful comment by Preston Manning, a Christian politician and former leader of a Canadian political party: "It is a mistake to see a moral issue where none exists but it is an even greater mistake to fail to see one where it does exist." Of course, we must also acknowledge that there are many political issues that are not really moral issues and about which religious people disagree.

3. We get involved because we know that silence does not create a situation of non-influence. Apathy and indifference can have devastating moral results. At this point we must acknowledge that for some Christians, and perhaps for all Christian citizens some of the time, non-involvement is a calculated stance taken for valid reasons. Nonetheless it is true that a major reason Adolf Hitler could continue his relentless persecution of the Jews was the almost total silence of the Christian church. We need

to remind ourselves that our moral responsibility is not set aside when we refuse to speak. We also realize that when we speak to government we are not thereby responsible for the policies the government ultimately adopts. We have done what we could.

4. We get involved because of our sense of stewardship. In most countries, people pay high taxes. In some, about half of the total national product flows through government hands at one level or another. Many of us have come to the conclusion that our Christian stewardship does not end after we pay our taxes—the 20 to 50 percent of our income that our various governments collect. If we have the opportunity to influence what is done with our tax money, at least some of us also have a responsibility to do so. At least some of us should provide suggestions and express concerns.

5. We get involved because even in the Palestine of biblical times, Jesus and some of his early followers did address social issues. In fact, we can go back as far as Mary's Magnificat and see a prophecy about Jesus addressing basic problems and needs (see Luke 1:46-55). James, the half-brother of Jesus, makes a compelling case for good works (see James 1:27; 2:14-26). We read, "Faith by itself, if it is not accompanied by action, is dead" (2:17). We also note Jesus' readiness to confront the civic-religious leaders of his day: "Woe to you, blind guides! . . . You hypocrites" (Matthew 23:16-36). Given our greater opportunities, we should be even more eager than Jesus' followers in the first century to express our concerns or encouragement, or both, as the situation may require.

6. We get involved because we should not divide our life into two different ethical sectors. We should not be like a cer-

tain Christian missionary to South Africa who, upon his return, reported that he had totally refrained from commenting on oppressive racial policies so that he could preach the gospel more easily. Does the gospel not address racism? William Templeton, Anglican theologian and Archbishop of Canterbury, has rightly observed, "It is a great mistake to suppose that God is only, or even mainly, concerned with religion."

In this connection I am reminded also of this poignant observation by the renowned Christian theologian M. Richard Shaull: "The question of bread for me is a material question; the question of bread for my neighbor is a spiritual matter."

7. In summary, we get involved because we are familiar with the biblical assertion that "righteousness exalts a nation" (Proverbs 14:34), and we want to do our part to make the political climate in our country as righteous as possible.

How and When Should Christians Get Involved?

We turn now to a discussion of the various levels and types of political involvement we may encounter. The most elementary form consists of becoming informed about what is happening politically. That is basic; how can we function as responsible Christian citizens if we are politically illiterate? How can we say that we take seriously the New Testament command—not suggestion—that we pray for our governments when we know practically nothing about them?

The logical next step is to convey our views directly to people in public office. While some Christians may not have the opportunity or inclination to do so, this is a very praiseworthy undertaking. Those Christian citizens who are not inclined or able to communicate their views personally can communicate indirectly by supporting organizations such as the Evangelical

Fellowship of Canada, the National Association of Evangelicals in the United States, the various councils of churches, Mennonite Central Committee, and many other fine agencies that routinely speak to the authorities.

The next level consists of voting. Surprisingly, some people think Christians should not vote. I respect them even though I see matters differently. These people tend to give one of three reasons: "My vote makes no difference"; "None of the candidates or parties appeals to me"; and "If I vote I'm more responsible for the outcome than if I don't vote." We can respond to these objections by stressing that every vote counts. Some elections have been determined by a handful of votes and, in a few instances, by only one vote. Second, even if there is no good option, it is still logical and commendable to choose the lesser evil. And third, neither voting nor refusing to vote makes one any more or less responsible for what politicians do later. The politicians are responsible for their actions; we are responsible for doing what we can.

A recent report by Christian evangelical author and minister Charles Colson indicated that in several congressional elections in the United States only about one-third of the evangelical Christians entitled to vote actually did so. This statistic is both surprising and disappointing in light of the major moral issues at stake in U.S. politics. The moral challenges in other countries are surely just as significant as are the moral challenges in the United States and therefore also warrant voter response. Granted, in a free society, the right to vote includes the right not to vote, but in my view the wise response by thoughtful citizens, especially Christian citizens, is to take advantage of the opportunity to vote.

Should Christians join political parties? I think that joining a political party is generally appropriate, provided that in doing so we do not agree to support an immoral or anti-Christian principle or a policy that restricts freedom in an unjustifiable manner. Members of parties often have considerable opportunity to influence policies. It is commendable if we utilize these. Of course, we must not try to link a particular party with the church or the cause of Christ, and we must be respectful of fellow Christians who choose to support a different political party or none at all.

Some Christians say that it is wasted effort to work for or join a political party because a party will never get rid of evil in society. True, parties are not geared to get rid of the sources of evil. That may be a spiritual issue, but through their elected members, parties have greatly improved society. They have brought an end to many bad policies and practices. For example, in many countries they have ended child labor, abolished slavery, reformed prisons, developed educational systems, provided hospitals and medical care, provided assistance for the destitute, and established free and fair courts. For most countries the list of what political parties have achieved is a long and impressive one. Many people ignore these successes and simply delight in criticizing political parties and denouncing politicians.

Obviously, in some respects political parties have not performed adequately. There is still much to be done. But let us not be overly critical. There is no perfect alternative to political action as a means to counteract the evil that persists in a fallen world. We should look at it this way: It is better that ethnic or tribal strife be at least partly suppressed than nothing be done. It is better that child abuse be cut in half than nothing be done. It is better that some government corruption is eliminated than nothing be done. It is better to have some prison reform than none. And it is surely better to have some opposition to organized crime than to let such criminals run amok. Political parties throughout the world, influenced by moral people, have done much that is praiseworthy.

Some Christians say that we should not join a political party because we should not be "yoked together with unbelievers" (2 Corinthians 6:14). But if we make no unchristian commitment in joining an interest group, business partnership, labor union, or political party, we are not "yoked" with unbelievers. Rather we can rightly see ourselves as a leaven to promote righteousness. Moreover, as we have noted, Christianity has a monopoly on salvation but not on compassion. It matters not to me if the person next to me in a bucket brigade fighting a house fire is a Muslim, an animist, or an atheist. We need that person to pass the bucket of water. We must cooperate to try to save the house! In a similar manner, Christians can work together with non-Christian politicians and others to do what is right. Church and government are not always in opposition, nor are Christian and non-Christian.

Should Christians become candidates for political office? While the issues here may loom larger, they are actually the same as when joining a political party or running for an office. The temptations to make unwise compromises may be greater, but the possibility of doing a lot of good may also be greater. Around the world, elected Christians have done much that is good. As a member of the British Parliament, William Wilberforce successfully led the campaign to abolish slavery in the United Kingdom. As a Mennonite Brethren member of the national government in Canada, Jake Epp initiated the successful campaign to abolish smoking on all commercial passenger airplanes. Doubtless much illness was prevented and many lives were saved as a result. Many other examples could be cited.

Christians who decide to seek political office should consider that Christian participation in politics is not driven by a quest for prestige or power. The motive is different. Jesus' call, no matter to what position in life, is a call to service, not to position. The position is the arena for service.

Society benefits from having Christians in political offices, but such leaders must respect certain guidelines. They must not commit their church to a political cause. They must not campaign in the church or use it to their political advantage. They must respect fellow Christians who have decided they cannot support a certain party or candidate. And they must not bring shame or disrepute to the cause of Christ. In addition, each Christian candidate or elected official would be well advised to establish a circle of close Christian friends, a trusted covenant community that can provide advice, guidance, and Christian correction. A Christian politician can check out policies, strategies, and plans with such a group, for there is usually wisdom in numbers. We repeat the basic axiom: in politics as in all other pursuits, Christians should never proceed further than Christian discipleship permits.

Similarly, it is highly commendable when Christians accept employment in governments, provided that they do not compromise their morals. Government service can be a fine place to spearhead moral initiatives and to demonstrate Christian ethics, including honesty, reliability, diligence, integrity, punctuality, good cheer, kindness, and sensitivity to people's situations. It is a good place to live out one's faith and even express it verbally. And in the many civil service situations in which employees are required to make decisions, government service is a good place to practice good judgment and the highest ethic to further the public good.

In all political activity, we citizens who bear the name of Christ should practice selective involvement. Not all political issues are worth a Christian citizen's time and energy. Not every problem requires a uniquely Christian response. Further, methods must always be consistent with goals. Dishonesty in trying to achieve something praiseworthy is still dishonesty.

Finally, it is improper and unchristian to try to use the coercive power of government to translate Christian morality into public policy. Of course, certain Christian principles and practices have such obvious general value that they have already been enacted into law; others likely will be in the future. The arm of the law enforces these policies. Christians have a right to suggest that certain Christian values should be enacted into law for the common good but should not press for legislation that is of benefit only for Christians. Christians should never use politics to gain benefits for themselves or for Christians generally at the expense of non-Christians.

A particular set of problems arises with reference to involvement in the military. For all Christians, but especially for those committed to nonviolence, ethical issues relating to taking human life must be faced. For many Christians the ethical tensions would be great. In times of military conscription, some Christian men and women have chosen the medical corps. Some have taken military training on condition that they will be involved only in peacekeeping assignments. Such choices should evoke respect and in many situations commendation. We must all allow for the reality that sincere Christians do come to differing conclusions concerning military service. These issues require extensive discussion that cannot be undertaken here. Suffice it to say that the ethical tensions relating to Christians choosing military involvement are different from those choosing other kinds of political activity and should not be seen as a reason for avoiding the usual civilian political activity.

Conclusion

The following statements may be useful as concluding observations.

- We do what we can in the political realm because we want to be found faithful. Too many Christians have too often privatized their convictions.
- Even though political involvement may not generate ultimate solutions, it often does produce improvement. We should not think in terms of "all or nothing." For example, governments may not be able to change the views of racists, especially in the short run, but they can prevent racist behavior. And over time, behavior will affect values.

- We must avoid the extremes of Constantinian captivity of the church—that is, the creation of a civic religion—and of the type of apathy that merely seeks to avoid any involvement.
- We must be careful not to underestimate or overestimate the potential of government for remedying evil or doing good. Similarly, as Michael Gerson has noted, "Christians in politics have to be idealists about goals and realists about means."
- Historically, some Christians, including many Anabaptists/ Mennonites, have stressed conscientious objection; the time has come to stress conscientious participation. We should reflect carefully on Dag Hammarskjöld's observation, "The way to holiness leads through action."
- Morally, politics is no different from many other kinds of activity undertaken mostly by non-Christians in a sub-Christian society.
- In political activity, party discipline and party ideology may cause a problem for Christians. There will be times when moral integrity will require Christians to terminate party memberships and Christian politicians to resign from political office. That, too, is effective witnessing.
- Thoughtful citizens are aware of a basic ethical dilemma. We need people with fixed and high moral principles to serve society in political offices, yet the essence of politics is compromise. Therefore, Christian politicians must pray for wisdom to know when to compromise and when not to compromise.
- Let us never try to limit the ways in which God may choose to work through one of his servants. In modern times as in history, God may call a Moses, a Mordecai, an Esther, a Daniel, or a Wilberforce to do his will.
- Concerning all political involvement, we join those parties and groups, we participate in those offices, we support those organizations and causes that permit us to practice Christian servanthood.

- We take to heart the words of an early American statesman, Benjamin Franklin: "He who shall introduce into public affairs the principles of Christianity will change the face of the world."
- We understand the wisdom in this statement of Martin Luther King Jr.: "A religion that ends with the individual, ends."
- And we heed the words of Edmund Burke: "All that is necessary for the triumph of evil is that good men do nothing."

8

The Overlapping Agendas of Church and Government

FOR MANY CENTURIES and in most of the world, governments have collected taxes, built roads, enforced law and order, fought wars, and undertaken various other forms of activity. For most people, the impact has been very consequential; sometimes it has been positive and sometimes very negative.

In most countries, a huge expansion of government services and programs has occurred in the last century. Some governments now provide social programs "from the cradle to the grave," as the saying goes. In some western countries, governments have created what some call a "nanny state," a state that functions almost like a parent or nanny. Even in those countries where financial resources are very limited, governments now undertake many more activities than in times past. Usually, in the wealthier as in the less wealthy lands, these initiatives have helped people to live better. Unfortunately, some government expansion has produced harsh and punitive policies, such as the manipulation of education, restriction of religious freedom, and undue interference in family life.

One thing is certain. Whether we live in economically developing countries or in the more developed lands, whether in former colonies or in former empires, we cannot escape the reality of growing government power and intervention. While the situation varies greatly from country to country, partly because of differing political systems and partly because of economic conditions, we all need to deal with this reality.

How should the Christian church as a whole and individual Christians react to this rapid growth of government? Should we welcome it? Should we resist it? Should we cooperate with governments? Should we not cooperate with governments? Should we work closely with the authorities when their programs mirror what Christians should be doing? Is government money tainted money?

Beginning with the Reformation era and for the following century, some Christian groups, including some Anabaptists, tried to avoid interaction and cooperation with governments. Given their theological view that the state is mostly evil and given the brutal treatment most governments meted out to them, such a negative stance by those groups was not surprising. As governments became more tolerant and as they adopted more enlightened policies, attitudes changed. In fact, in recent decades some of us in the Anabaptist tradition have taken the view that in some situations we should be partners with government in doing good deeds. For some Anabaptists and some other Christians, that is a radical idea. Is government not outside of the kingdom of God? Let us now analyze the arguments, pro and con, concerning cooperation with governments by the church and church agencies.

Why the Church and Government Should Cooperate

Why should churches and church agencies sometimes cooperate with governments? Here are five important reasons.

First, as already noted, in many countries, governments have taken over projects that churches and church agencies pioneered. The establishment of schools, hospitals, orphanages, homes for the aged, hostels, and "poor houses" that gave food to the hungry are some examples. Why should we not be helping our governments do what Christians have done for centuries and what Christians continue to do?

Second, the money governments spend is largely tax money that once belonged to us, the taxpayers. If we can help our government to use some of our money as wisely as possible, we should do so. Many Christian and other private agencies can use our tax monies much more efficiently than can governments. Such utilizations of funds can be seen as expanded Christian stewardship. And we can still try to influence how our money is used by government agencies.

Third, in many areas of service, such as sponsoring refugees, providing for the homeless, and reacting to natural catastrophes, we can help our government to be more humanitarian and more responsive to human need. Christians can make government aid more compassionate and personal. As the salt of the earth, as the conscience of society, the church functions as a force for good. Working with government can be another arena in which the Christian church expresses love and compassion, an undertaking in which Christians collectively do what the good Samaritan did for a waylaid traveler who desperately needed help (see Luke 10:29-37). We can be especially influential here by setting good examples. This has often been done. Churches have sponsored refugees, provided overseas assistance, offered emergency aid, and undertaken many other fine services and then encouraged government agencies to do likewise. Leading by example is an excellent way for Christians to influence government policies.

Fourth, many churches have themselves benefited much from various forms of government aid. In fact, many Christian groups and denominations continue to ask governments for assistance and even special favors. Such favors have involved exemption from taxation, granting of clergy benefits, use of affirmation instead of oaths, recognition of Christian schools, and reduction of taxes because of charitable donations. The benefits may also include other-oriented actions, such as approval for overseas aid, the licensing of local charity endeavors, the availability of government grants for religious hospitals, the availability of grants for homes for the elderly, and other similar ministries.

Some Christian groups have asked for and often received some truly amazing government benefits. For example, many Quakers, Mennonites, and others received exemption from military service as conscientious objectors. Some Christian groups were given extensive government help in family reunification. Some received land grants. And some were allowed special language and religious instruction in their own schools.

It is probably appropriate and justifiable for religious groups to have such close relations with government and to have governments extend benefits to them. But precisely because of this record of benefits, Christians need to take seriously the opportunity of working with governments for the benefit of others. Christianity, after all, is other-oriented.

Fifth, governments need many good people to help carry out policies. For example, governments benefit when they can work with reliable, honest, and conscientious agencies, such as the Salvation Army, Mennonite Central Committee, and World Vision, to deliver assistance to needy people at home and abroad, and to hand out government assistance in times of natural disaster. It can be argued that such cooperation with government in serving society can be seen as another form of Christian ministry.

Christians know that government is an agency established by God to serve society and to do what is good (see Romans 13:1-7). The church and other Christian agencies should therefore utilize opportunities to help the government carry out its God-given mandate, to be a better government for the people. Thus, when we help governments to be better governments, we are serving God.

Opposition to Church-Government Cooperation

Those Christians who believe that the church should not cooperate with governments, even in carefully selected policies and programs, can also list some important reasons. Their concerns need to be weighed carefully. Let us review the five main objections.

First, the Christian church has more important things to do. Let the people of the world do the deeds of the world, even the good deeds of the world. The church has a different and higher mandate. As I see it, the situation is as follows: Yes, the main purpose of the church is to carry out a higher calling but that need not exclude other activities. In fact, the higher calling actually includes doing good works. Accordingly, leaders of the church and of church agencies need to decide in each instance whether a particular partnership with government, working at overlapping agendas, can be seen as an extension of the church's calling to do good deeds or whether it is a distraction. They need to decide whether such involvement can be seen as the fruit of the gospel. Clearly, not every overture from government deserves a positive response from the Christian church. But more than a few do.

Second, most people in politics are not Christians, and government itself is not a Christian agency living by a Christian ethic. For that reason the church and church agencies should not cooperate with government, even when we have similar goals. My response is that the Christian church must be very careful about forming a partnership, even a limited cooperative undertaking, with any sub-Christian agency. But there are times when we go into the world as Jesus did and interact closely with the world in order to minister to the world. After all, the church has been called to be active in the world even though it is not of the world.

Third, if a government is dictatorial, evil, or brutal, and if it does not grant freedom to the churches, we should have nothing to do with it. Such involvement, the argument goes, would not do the church any good and would serve only the cause of unjust rulers. Moreover, it would be detrimental also in the sense that it would be seen as giving legitimacy to something evil. As I see it, such a response is natural and understandable and has considerable merit. However, by working with even an evil government in some carefully selected undertakings, we are reinforcing that which is good and perhaps causing the government to reevaluate policies that are unwise or evil. Further, if we help and affirm when we can, we can with greater credibility criticize when we must.

Fourth, various political parties, and sometimes military or revolutionary movements as well, are all competing via elections or in other ways to become the government of the land. By identifying with one of them, the church would be taking sides and hurting its witness to other groups. In fact, it is argued, such a church might even create problems for itself in the future because a time will likely come when some other political party or military force, previously opposed by the church, will take office. The church could then find itself in difficulty.

There is some validity in this argument, but it is not an insurmountable objection. If the church does not get involved in partisan campaigning or official party endorsements but only affirms good policies dealing—for example, with racism, refugee assistance, or the sanctity of traditional marriage—it has not compromised its integrity. It would support such policies in any party or movement. If the church or Christian agency clearly states that it is open to limited cooperation with any government that undertakes good policies, there should be no negative consequences. There may be some risks, but courageous Christian ministry and witnessing often involves risk.

Fifth, if churches accept government funds for their own or joint projects, they may soon become dependent on such funds and the projects might collapse if the government suddenly ends its support. This is a valid concern. However, if the undertaking involves meeting urgent social needs, the government is very unlikely to end its support or partnership, because to do so would likely leave an even greater problem on its own doorstep. Thus a government is not likely to cut off assistance to a church-sponsored home for the elderly, causing it to fail and thereby returning the responsibility to that government.

Concerning other undertakings not seen to be addressing urgent needs, government funding can end at any time, either because of changing government priorities or because a government is replaced. Churches should never allow a truly important part of the Christian mandate, such as international aid, to become dependent on government money or a government partnership. Government funding, with or without active government participation, should therefore probably be used only for short-term, special, or extra ministries.

Sixth, it is argued that sometimes the government puts conditions on its support or partnership that churches find unacceptable. I would reply that in those cases the churches or church agencies are well advised not to proceed with the joint or government-funded project. Let it be said again that when we encourage churches to work with governments in certain projects, we are speaking only of those where no such problem exists.

Finding a Middle Ground

In evaluating these arguments, churches and church agencies in all lands must reach their own conclusions. There is a time to act and a time not to act. There is a time to take government money and a time not to take government money. In some lands, churches have gone so far as almost to fuse their identity and mission with that of their government or even their country. Such a stance is unwise and theologically unwarranted. Some other church groups have gone to the other extreme and have tried to cut off any connection to government. This, too, strikes me as unfortunate. We need balance. Concerning involvement in the political realm, especially in cooperative ventures, churches and church agencies should follow the rule of caution and of limited and selective involvement. Although churches need to tread very cautiously in these areas, I see a significant opportunity in carefully selected cooperation with government.

Let us recall that in many countries, churches and their agencies have not hesitated to work with governments to achieve benefits for themselves. The fact that many churches and agencies may not have acknowledged such actions to be political does not change the fact that they were. When something advances our own interests, we sometimes put a particularly positive label on it. Governments have helped churches with matters such as family unification, language privileges, education privileges, military exemption for conscientious objectors, settlement assistance, favorable zoning, exemption from paying property taxes, and other benefits. We should not object to such activity. In fact, we do well to selectively and carefully extend the list of endeavors. But we also need to focus on using our interaction with government to serve the needs of others.

In some countries, including Canada, the United Kingdom, and the United States, an impressive list of successful church-government cooperative ventures has developed. While many projects have focused mainly on helping churches, others have been undertaken to help disadvantaged groups and individuals in the homeland and abroad. Permit me to review part of the Canadian record.

The Canadian International Development Agency (CIDA) has encouraged churches and church members to donate grain for overseas relief and has doubled or, with the help of some provincial governments, even quadrupled the amount of grain farmers donated for shipment to needy people overseas. Many Christian farmers have taken advantage of this opportunity to help the needy. Huge amounts of grain have been sent, while some has been sold and the money has been sent. Sometimes this donation of grain by farmers is done through the Foodgrains Bank, basically a Christian charity; sometimes it is done through other agencies. Many hungry people have been fed. Perhaps we should see this highly successful cooperation between church agency and government as a new form of "feeding the five thousand" (see Matthew 14:15-21).

Aside from the CIDA grain project, the Canadian government has for decades made available to the Mennonite Central Committee (MCC) and other church aid groups huge amounts of surplus food at little or no cost. The government stores the staples, usually powdered milk and eggs, and the religious agencies provides the personnel to get the food shipments to their destinations. This cooperation has helped hundreds of thousands of people living in many countries—a second contemporary equivalent of "feeding the five thousand."

The Canadian government also has established a program whereby MCC has been able to sponsor thousands of desperate refugees. The government and MCC have supported one another with mutual encouragement for even greater assistance to refugees. Many Mennonite churches, along with others also, provide hosting, training, and general assistance to the newcomers. For more than twenty years this arrangement has been a win-win situation for all, but especially for the refugees.

In addition, for almost a hundred years Mennonite churches in Canada have worked closely with the Canadian government to reunite families split by wars. The government has been very helpful, but it has also benefited because it has gained many thousands of fine citizens.

Most of the ten provincial governments in Canada have provided funds for Christian schools operated by Christian groups. Generally, these funds are not for capital construction, but they usually do provide about 50 percent of the per student operating grants given to public schools. Thus the private schools get half as much as the public schools get. In this win-win situation, churches have been able to operate schools that incorporate their particular religious values as well as the required curriculum, and the government has not had to pay the much greater costs which would result if all the students in these private Christian schools were enrolled in public schools.

At both provincial and national levels, governments have provided loans, grants, and scholarships to enable young people to study in Christian post-secondary schools. This practice is also common in the United States. These students have even been permitted to study theology and other Christian subjects in preparation for Christian ministry. Many Christian taxpayers are pleased to see some of their tax monies spent this way.

Several church agencies, including MCC, also have worked jointly with governments to provide a better life for native Canadians, the aboriginal people whom we used to call Indians. Again, thousands have been helped.

In both World Wars, the American and Canadian governments worked with Mennonite and other church groups to provide alternative service for conscientious objectors, draftees who rejected military service. Although about half of the Mennonite young men who were drafted chose military service, including the medical corps, thousands of others welcomed the alternative options. Some worked in hospitals, some in forests, some on roads, some in Goodwill centers and some on farms. They earned virtually no wages, but they did contribute in a positive way to society. In both the United States and Canada such alternative service was also made available for young men drafted during peacetime.

For the past half-century or more, state, provincial and national governments have provided large financial grants to church groups for the operation and construction of hospitals, homes for seniors, and other healthcare facilities. This has been a very rewarding partnership, and many thousands of people, Christian as well as others, have been helped.

These examples illustrate my point. Other examples that could be cited deal with food banks for the hungry, employment centers, recycling operations, educational programs for immigrants, day care and nursery programs, housing projects, as well as housing and programs for people with physical or mental disabilities. Such examples abound in the United States, in Canada, and in various other countries.

In all these undertakings, the overlapping interests and agendas of church and government have produced major benefits for society. While many of the programs still focus mainly on benefiting the church communities themselves and although some churches remain suspicious of such joint activity, much that is truly excellent has already been accomplished.

Of course, in other countries the situation will be different, the needs will vary, and in some places resources may be very scarce. However, opportunities for church-government cooperation probably exist in almost every country, province, and city. Whether in a developed or a developing country, a faithful church committed to cooperate with political authorities for the common good will find suitable avenues of involvement.

We have briefly surveyed some actual areas of overlapping agendas in Canada and the United States, largely developed countries. In other developed countries, the areas of overlapping agendas and issues of joint interest are similar. What might be the overlapping agendas of church and government in a developing country? They might include health education, ministry to refugees, prison visitation, environmental cleanup, safety patrolling, hospital help, various forms of tutoring, assistance for AIDS orphans, emergency relief, and literacy programs. Each church and agency would have to take stock of its resources and investigate local or regional needs. Over the years I have been surprised at how open governments have been when a private organization, typically a Christian church or a church-related agency, comes with a specific and realistic proposal and offers to help. Governments don't hear such proposals very often.

Conclusion

Let me offer some general observations. First, although church-state cooperation holds considerable promise for Christian ministry, it must not detract from that part of the great commission that exhorts Christians to proclaim the gospel of salvation to all people. The two emphases can and should proceed simultaneously. Words and deeds together encompass what Jesus commanded his followers to do.

Second, church-government cooperation, two agents of God working at common agendas, is an important fruit of the gospel. Some churches need to move beyond an "us/them" mindset and look for ways to work in community with those who, perhaps without being aware of the differences, function according to another ethic but according to Romans 13 are servants of God in the other order. Christians also need to remind themselves that all citizens, Christian and non-Christian, are part of the political order, and when we work at improving the political order and try to help it serve God more obediently, we are helping both ourselves and others.

Third, as the scope of government continues to increase, the question becomes not *if* church and government should interact but *how* they should do so. My plea is that the interaction includes a large measure of working together at common agendas. Often this is done most effectively at the local level; at other times, as with the Canadian Foodgrains Bank, it is done best at the national level.

Fourth, churches and their agencies, like individual Christians, function in both of God's orders. Religious activity in the more important order, the church, will be enhanced if Christians also minister in the other one, the political.

Finally, churches sometimes are caught up with being critical of the political realm. As we all know, there is certainly much about which to be critical and there is a place for such criticism. But let us move beyond criticism. As I see it, we do better in the eyes of man and God if, when a negative response is timely, it is accompanied by positive action.

9

Can Morality Be Legislated? Should Christians Practice Pressure Politics?

THE QUESTIONS THAT SERVE as the title of this chapter have been debated for a long time, and the debates continue. Some Christians argue that morality cannot be legislated, that no government action can change bad people into good people. Other Christians argue that government does have the ability —indeed, the responsibility—to improve human behavior. Can both groups be right? And if the latter view is correct, do Christians have an obligation to pressure governments to do a better job?

Legislating Morality

Let us look at the first question. In the narrow meaning of the word *legislate,* it is correct to say that governments cannot legislate morality. Morality deals with motives, matters of the heart, internal values. Governments, on the other hand, deal with behavior, with external actions. Governments cannot, by enacting law, suddenly change people's motives or values. Their mandate is to regulate and control behavior, particularly as it impacts people. But that's not the end of the story. I suggest that laws, regulations, and court decisions do influence and often shape morality over time. Let me explain.

In the famous 1954 U.S. Supreme Court decision *Brown v. Board of Education,* the court ruled that "separate but equal" schools for white and black children were not, in fact, equal and that it was illegal for school boards to have such a policy in place. The court ruled that public schools should be integrated. The new policy was then gradually enforced. Many school boards across the country and large segments of the American public, especially in the southern states, disagreed strongly with this decision. However, they had no choice but to accept complete, although gradual, integration of the public schools. They were forced to change their public behavior, even though they did not change their beliefs and values.

Eventually, attitudes changed. As opponents saw that integration could work, minds and values began to shift. Within a few decades, black and white children had grown up knowing nothing but integrated schools. At the same time, the number of school board members and parents who opposed this court-ordered integration dropped sharply. By about 1980, virtually no one in the entire United States was still arguing in favor of racially segregated schools. What had happened? By legislating and enforcing changed behavior, over time the political authorities brought about a change in attitudes, motives, and value systems. In that sense, morality was legislated.

I might add that as more than a few American Christians look back at *Brown v. Board of Education,* they are embarrassed by the fact that in many places it was the government, not the church, that took the lead in challenging racism in public schools. In fact, in some states, evangelical Christians put up very strong resistance to racial integration.

Evangelical Christians have traditionally been inclined to say that moral change occurs when sinners come to Christ. They are obviously right. At least that's the way it should be according to biblical teaching. But it was not the mass conversion of people to Christianity that precipitated the end of segregation in the United States. Time and again we have seen that improved morality can also be achieved, although in most cases only gradually, by enlightened government policies. Perhaps this same effect occurs in the training of children. When parents force a child to say please and thank you, within a few years the child *wants* to do so. Over time, guided or enforced behavior changes internal values. People can be trained, educated, and pressured to become more moral.

Another informative example involves the institution of slavery. In the United Kingdom, the United States, Canada, and numerous other countries, slavery was gradually made illegal by governments that forced the issue. In the United Kingdom William Wilberforce did not have majority public support as he and his associates cajoled and pressured the British government to abolish the system. In some countries, including the United States, feelings ran strong. In the United States the differences ran so deep that civil war resulted. What has happened since that time? Although modern slavery does, unfortunately, exist in certain places, I would venture to guess that in all of the United Kingdom, the United States, and Canada, and in various other countries we would have difficulty finding any people who support slavery other than a few neo-Nazis and similar extremists who come close to doing so. What brought about this incredible shift of opinion? Government legislation and action played the major role.

So, as has been documented many times in political history, we see that governments can enact policies that change public opinion and improve human behavior. We now turn to a study of activity intended to influence governments. This analysis applies primarily to open and democratic societies, but it also has relevance for those societies not yet fully democratic.

We should not underestimate or overestimate the ability of governments to remedy social ills. We need to be realistic. Governments can sometimes achieve significant changes in public behavior, but there is much that governments cannot do. They cannot and should not force people to become Christians or legislate love for one's neighbor. Governments also cannot control people's thoughts and beliefs, and should not attempt to do so. Neither should they invade people's privacy and try to regulate activity that does not harm other people or the public in any way. Boundary issues arise, to be sure, as with the "right" to commit suicide or forms of deviant sexual behavior. These need to be addressed in an enlightened and fair manner.

What About a 'Social Gospel'?

We need to say a word here about the so-called social gospel. For generations Christians throughout the world have debated how evangelism and social action should relate to one another. Should they both be pursued? Are they of equal importance? This dichotomizing of the Christian witness is unfortunate. The life and teachings of Christ clearly show that he was interested in total people, in their spiritual as well as their physical well-being. Christians should be, too. In Matthew 5:16 Jesus says, "Let your light shine before men, that they may see your good deeds and praise your Father in heaven." The book of James stresses the same truth forcefully: "As the body without the spirit is dead, so faith without works is dead" (James 2:26).

Further, in Matthew 25 Jesus describes his followers as being those who feed the hungry, give drink to the thirsty, give clothes to the naked, host strangers, look after the sick, and visit those who are in prison. Here we have an amazingly powerful affirmation by Jesus himself of social action. In sum, what many evangelicals have rejected as "the social gospel" is described here by Jesus as the test of true Christian discipleship.

We might note that in preaching this truth, Jesus was incorporating the forceful teaching of the Old Testament prophets. According to Micah 6:8, "He has showed you, O man, what is good. And what does the Lord require of you? To act justly and to love mercy and to walk humbly with your God." Isaiah 1:16-17 states the same truth.

Does a strong evangelical thrust go together with a commitment to help the needy and pursue justice? Perhaps Christians should not even be asking the question! Christians should know that these two endeavors go hand in hand, as in Jesus' own ministry. What he modeled, we should also do.

Let's consider another truth. Christians should acknowledge that, whatever they do, they proclaim a social gospel to the world. If Christians do nothing to help the needy, that is their social gospel. They are saying that they are unconcerned and uninterested in their neighbors' plight. Thus it is not a matter of *whether* Christians have a social gospel but of *what kind* of social gospel they have.

Pressing the Government for Change

We turn now to the topic of pressuring governments to do what is right. Should Christian activists and lobbyists act alone? Is there a place in Christian discipleship for group activity to achieve greater justice and decency in government policies and actions? Which methods would be appropriate? While much practical Christian activity to address evil and injustice can and should be undertaken in the private sector, some of it can only be done effectively in the political arena. Let us now analyze the matter.

Some Christians—actually quite a few—have argued that to participate in any political pressure groups (also called lobbies) is morally questionable or even wrong. Let me explain

why I cannot agree with that view. The existence and operation of pressure groups—whether educational, religious, business, labor, agricultural, environmental, or others—is a mark
of a healthy political system. To have pressure groups is to
enjoy freedom of opinion and expression. In an oppressive dictatorship, all pressure groups are either banned or fully controlled. Pressure groups provide an important service in providing feedback to rulers. Sometimes they work only to
advance their own narrow interests, but often they have gotten
governments to adopt good policies that might not otherwise
have been adopted. They also function as safety valves, as a
means whereby people can vent their feelings without resort-
ing to violence. It is surely much better to express your views
and grievances to governments verbally than to undertake
physical resistance.

All enlightened governments welcome pressure-group
input. It helps them to discover what is bothering their citizens, it provides much new information, and it helps them to
be more accountable. Pressure groups thus play an important
and very useful role in society. Let me go a step further. I
would argue that if carried out properly, pressure-group activity can be a form of Christian witness. In fact, I know of many
instances in which government officials have been very grateful for the input provided by Christian pressure groups, such
as the National Association of Evangelicals, the Evangelical
Fellowship of Canada, the Christian Leadership Conference,
the National Council of Churches, the Canadian Conference
of Catholic Bishops, the Committee on Justice and Liberty,
Evangelicals for Social Action, Prison Fellowship, Liberty
Alliance, and scores of other. I have observed that government
officials are especially receptive and grateful when Christian
groups press for benefits for others rather than for themselves.
Relatively few other political activists do that. Christian pressure groups have been effective in bringing about prison
reform, better treatment of refugees, fairer distribution of wel-

fare aid, intervention in areas of religious persecution, greater freedoms for minority groups, and many other gains.

Not all Christians are impressed by the historical record. Some ask why Christians should get involved in trying to deal with the problems of an unchristian world. Why deal with symptoms instead of focusing on the root cause of evil? Why deal only with the consequences of rejecting God instead of trying to end the rejection? These questions deserve answers.

Let me list some reasons I believe that such political involvement is commendable, especially for Christians organized into groups outside of the formal church structures, although sometimes the evil to be challenged is so grievous that the official church should speak. Though such groups may be small, fortunately they do exist, and they are needed. Unfortunately, some Christians think that all pressure and lobbying activity should be prohibited, and that is the issue that needs to be addressed.

Christians do try to reverse people's rejection of God, and that is paramount. But like God himself, Christians also pay attention to situations in which people of their own free will choose not to submit to God. The compassion of these Christians, just like God's, extends to all people in this fallen world. Christians are called to bring Christian concerns to bear on all people, all institutions, and all power levels. No level of decision making must be allowed to escape from the judgment of God. In addition to the great commission, which calls for an experiential relationship with God, Christianity also includes what some term a "cultural mandate," that is, an obligation to penetrate society to improve it.

Christians are not chaplains sent to soothe the consciences of unjust rulers. At times Christians should disturb consciences, not calm them. Christians recall that Jesus challenged the evil deeds of theocratic authorities in his day and performed many practical deeds of kindness (see, for example, Matthew 9:35; 21:12-17).

Of course, Jesus had a very special calling, lived a short life, and had time for little else. He also lived in a dictatorship, and therefore his challenge to evil authorities was mostly indirect. Given the opportunities of our modern democracies, our challenges can be much more extensive and need not be indirect.

The presentation of the gospel and the witness to the state are interrelated; indeed they are continuous. Consider Paul's appearance before Felix in Acts 24, John the Baptist's challenge to Herod and Herodias in Matthew 14 and Mark 6, and Peter's response to the Sanhedrin in Acts 4 and 5. Christians today are called to do likewise.

When Christians know how to do good and do not do it, they are guilty of the sin of omission (see James 4:17). Many Christians possess the knowledge and personal skills to serve others as part of a Christian pressure group in the political realm. When opportunities present themselves, do these Christians not have an obligation to advocate for a truly worthy cause?

Christians are not to focus only on the needs of fellow believers, important as those needs should be for us. They are to be good neighbors to others, like the good Samaritan (see Luke 10:25-29). Jesus praised the good Samaritan lavishly for ministering to a total stranger of a different ethnic group and for providing material help and apparently saying not one word to him. The world is full of needy people who need such help. We try to help them individually, but sometimes the challenge involves more than just one person helping another. Sometimes a government must be pressured to act because it is itself the cause of the problem. Sometimes the problem is so large—international drug smuggling, for example—that only the government has the resources to deal with it. At times, only governments are in a position to address the needs of large masses of people. In such situations, Christian pressure groups can play a key role in urging governments to act and can often work with government agencies to get the task done.

Christians stand up for what is right in order to enhance Christian credibility. The political realm is an arena that presents such opportunity. Peter emphasizes the positive impact of good deeds: "For it is God's will that by doing good you should silence the ignorant talk of foolish men" (1 Peter 2:15). Note also verse 12: "Live such good lives among the pagans that, though they accuse you of doing wrong, they may see your good deeds and glorify God on the day he visits us." Many Christians have done good deeds in the political realm, either as individuals or as members of pressure groups. More Christians should take them as models.

The Christian church can be many things, but it cannot be irrelevant. Silence and inaction also speak loudly. The moral acquiescence of the church carries great weight. Christians know that moral responsibility is not avoided when they refuse to speak while governments carry out evil policies.

A Christian, indeed the whole Christian church, cannot be faithful to Christ's calling without being the leaven of discontent when such discontent is needed. In the case of policies like apartheid and racial segregation, such leaven is required. In such situations, group expression is often more effective than individual responses.

Christians believe, or ought to believe, that by working with others they can make society fairer, more humanitarian, and more civilized. Past achievements should be an encouragement. Christians want to promote freedom and human dignity. When they speak with a collective voice about such matters, they are more readily heard and heeded than if they speak individually.

Christians get involved because they are familiar with the biblical guidelines for government as described in Romans 13 and elsewhere. It has been said that the faithful Christian church is the conscience of society. Maybe the Christian church, perhaps speaking through group structures, can also function as the conscience of government.

Luther looked to the state to help preserve the church; Calvin looked to the church to help preserve and guide the state; the early Anabaptists believed that the church should witness to the state. In our day, Christians can both witness verbally and serve in capacities that Christian discipleship permits and thereby enhance the well-being of both church and state.

Guidelines for Speaking to Government

When Christians speak to rulers and public officials about political matters, whether as individuals or in groups, what values and ethics should guide them? As much as possible, Christians try to be positive rather than negative. Governments are already almost overwhelmed with complaints and criticisms. They need help rather than more condemnation. In their interaction with rulers, Christians should always reflect the biblical emphasis on being supportive, when that is possible, and tactfully critical, when that is appropriate.

Rulers typically argue that the Christian ethic is not relevant for them, perhaps because they are not Christians or perhaps because politics in this fallen world simply requires a different ethic. Moreover, the optimal ethic for governments, some argue, is justice, not love. Be that as it may, Christians can still demonstrate the utilitarian value of the Christian ethic for everyone and try to get as much of it accepted as is appropriate. When Christians cannot achieve the best, they work to achieve the good, or the second best, because it is better than the bad. They do so because they believe that governing can be improved even though governments do not accept Christ's lordship.

Christians never ask the government to use the arm of the law to help carry out the great commission. But Christians can and should urge government to use the arm of the law to combat evils, including many that the Bible identifies and that have been incorporated into official legislation and regulation.

Not every political issue requires a uniquely Christian response. In fact, not every one requires *any* Christian response. Many political issues fall below the Christian's priority cut-off line. While it may be incumbent for Christians in the political system to express their views on a wide range of mundane and non-moral issues, the church or the Christian community may not have anything distinctive to say on the issues and need not address them.

When Christians communicate to governments through pressure groups, what is their agenda? What should they ask governments to do? While the specific items will vary from time to time and from country to country, the following general concerns should be remembered.

- Christians should work to achieve strong guarantees for broad freedoms, including religious freedom. Christians should urge that these freedoms be extended to all groups and individuals, including those with whose religious views they disagree, provided that such groups respect the operating rules of a free society. Christians want no coercion in religious matters, not even coercion in support of Christianity. They desire freedom and the opportunity to carry out their mandate.
- Christians should press for more justice in the courts, in regulatory agencies, in government boards and tribunals, and in civil service. The fact that Christians may themselves be the immediate or even dominant beneficiaries does not negate or minimize the broader good. Christians are part of the larger society and have every right to seek its well-being.
- Christians should urge governments to eliminate corruption, to practice honesty and integrity, and to uphold fairness in procedures and justice in their decisions. In these

matters Christians should be the most alert and the most observant watchdogs. In this as in all other areas, Christian pressure groups owe the government a commitment to speak the truth as they see it, diplomatically but also boldly. Of course, they should also lead by example in this and other areas.

•Christians should press for prison reform. The New Testament has much to say about this, with Jesus expressing deep concern for prisoners. It has well been said, "Show me the state of your prisons and I will tell you the moral state of your country." Chuck Colson's organization has a stellar record in such ministry and service. He and his prison ministry enjoy amazing effectiveness and credibility precisely because of the record that this ministry has established.

•Christians should not try to get the government to be the church. The responsibilities are different. Nevertheless, Christian pressure groups should urge the government to seek and to pursue peace.

•Christians remind governments of their constitutional obligations, their electoral promises, and their duty to govern for the general good. In particular, Christian pressure groups provide advice and suggestions in those areas where they have demonstrated expertise or where they have modeled what they would like governments to do, for example, in compassionate treatment of refugees and in treating the environment with proper care and respect.

•Finally, Christian pressure groups remind rulers that they are ultimately accountable to the great divine Ruler.

When to Speak Up
When should Christian pressure groups speak to government? What conditions should prompt the expression of concerns or other comments?

- Christians speak when rulers command them or others to disobey God.
- Christians speak when rulers invite them to comment or give advice.
- Christians speak when rulers become arbitrary and exceed their constitutional restraints.
- Christians speak words of commendation when government action is worthy of support or praise. Christians thank and compliment when they can so that they can criticize with credibility when they must.
- Christians speak when a government is grossly inconsistent or arbitrary in its application of rules and regulations.
- Christians speak when a government persistently ignores major societal problems and evils even though it has the means to address them.
- Christians speak when governments are unresponsive to the legitimate concerns of minorities and exploited individuals.
- Christians speak when governments, including courts, undermine human dignity and oppose fundamental God-ordained institutions such as traditional marriage and the family.
- Christians speak when governments affirm the killing of the most innocent and vulnerable human beings by abortion.

In getting involved in the political arena as members of pressure groups, Christians very soon face the question of whether they should work together with non-Christian pressure groups. Obviously, they should be cautious. Christians must not compromise their ethics and must not bring disrespect on their church. But equally important is the potential of working with people of other faiths or people of no faith so that more good can be achieved. Christians do not have a monopoly on compassion, on moral indignation, or on political insight. Christian pressure groups opposing slavery, for example, have worked closely with non-Christian groups to pressure governments to legislate an end to this great evil.

In undertaking lobbying or otherwise urging governments to do what is right, all pressure groups, and certainly Christian ones, must be careful to use proper methods. The means should never undermine the ends. Christian political activists should always be respectful, kind, patient, friendly, and reasonable. They should be good listeners. They should also be willing to accept reasonable compromises on nonessentials. Given political realities, they should be willing to accept the improvement of society by degrees.

Conclusion

In conclusion, let me underscore a few general observations. Although it is very important, political involvement, including pressure group activity as we have analyzed it here, is secondary to living a godly life and to proclaiming the need for salvation in Christ. Further, while there are major overlapping agendas and many common areas of interest, selective involvement is important. Only certain political issues, especially those where Christians have themselves modeled what can and should be done, warrant attention by Christians. The most effective witness the church can express to society and to political rulers is to be a truly faithful church, modeling in society what Jesus taught and practiced.

10

Can There Be a Christian Political Party? Is Christianity Left, Right, or Center?

IN MANY COUNTRIES, Christian citizens have formed so-called Christian political parties. Usually the word *Christian* appears in the name of the party, as in Canada's Christian Heritage Party. These parties have generally not won elections except where the party has kept the name but has set aside authentic Christian teaching. It has not yet been demonstrated that a party fully committed to biblical teaching can win at the polls in modern times.

Many observers believe that Christians should not organize as a political party in order to seek electoral victory as a way of implementing Christian truth. At least two fundamental reasons are given. First, such a tactic is divisive. Christian citizens hold widely differing beliefs concerning which set of values a government should implement. As we will see shortly, Christians tend to lean toward liberal, conservative, or socialist views, depending on which part of the gospel is being emphasized. Second, and much more important, the church and a political party have different mandates, purposes, scopes, methods, ethical norms, and goals.

The following comparative chart highlights the extensive contrasts.

Item	Church	Political Party
Highest virtue	Love	Justice
General orientation	Other-oriented	Self-oriented
Basic purpose	Carrying out the great commission	Gaining power and implementing its policies
Method of operation	Persuasion	Ultimately coercion (if in government)
Sources of authority	God; the Bible	Elites or public majority; usually a constitution
Sources of morality	God; the Bible	Public preference; party policy; leaders' views
Nature of basic ethics	Absolutist, altruistic	Compromise; majority views; pragmatism
Scope of constituency	The world; a global family of believers	One country or a jurisdiction within it
Attitude to religion	Proclamation of one true faith	Equality of all faiths or supremacy of one faith
Constituency; membership	Christian believers	All people in one country or a jurisdiction in it
Final goal	Glorification of God	Progress and security through party policies

It is possible, indeed desirable, for political parties to embrace many Christian values. Many Christian virtues are desirable as public policies not because they are Christian but because they have general utilitarian value; they are intrinsically good for society. Christian members in political parties can play a vital role in having this understood. Christian influence has been widespread during the last few centuries, infusing many a political policy with considerable enlightenment and virtue. But we should not think that Christians operating as a political party in the political realm can achieve the fundamental purpose for which Jesus established the church he heads.

Conceivably, a group of Christians could establish a totally Christian political party. If true to its values, it could function as a useful gadfly, even in a fallen, sub-Christian society. In fact, it could be quite effective as the conscience of the entire political system. Some small parties have come reasonably close to achieving that role, although important compromises have usually been made to gain wider approval among voters.

It is very problematic for the Christian church, or even a segment of it, to function as a political party, even if it is an opposition party and thus not in government. In my view, it is impossible for it to be true to a biblical calling if it gains political power. The Christian ethic puts the welfare of others ahead of one's own; political parties campaigning to be elected do not do so. The church does not employ coercion; the state does. In realistic terms, a truly Christian political party would have to cease to operate fully according to the Christian ethic and would have to set aside a strictly biblical purpose if it were ever elected to form the government.

Nonetheless, some Christians have argued that there should be a thoroughly biblical political party as an option for voters in a free society. It could at least function as a symbol of the ideal. Indeed, that could be a useful role as it sacrifices influence and perhaps power for principle. Some proponents further argue that since the principles of such Christian parties incorporate key biblical values, individual Christians—not the church as a church body—should support such parties. That assertion is hotly debated.

Assessing Secular Political Parties

We turn now to an evaluation of the ideologies of mainstream political parties. Unfortunately, there is no agreement among Christian observers or political activists concerning which of the largely secular political ideologies is most worthy of Christian support. Typically, across the western world, the attempted association involves parties based on conservatism, liberalism, or socialism. To ascertain the extent to which any given party or ideology actually correlates with Christian values, we need to become familiar with the principles and policies of each of the three dominant ideologies. In various countries the parties espousing these ideologies take on a variety of names, some of which can be misleading. In this survey we are assessing actual ideologies, not party names.

Since there is not space here to spell out the history of each ideology, I will concentrate on the main assumptions and values of each as I compare it to conservative, orthodox Christianity.

Conservatism

Conservative Christianity and political conservatism share some important emphases. Both stress individualism and individual responsibility within a larger community that possesses significant organic unity, whether church or nation. Christian conservatism emphasizes personal conscience, personal salvation, personal morality, personal service in God's kingdom, and personal accountability to God. Political conservatism stresses personal moral responsibility, personal initiative, substantial but not total personal responsibility for one's economic well-being, and personal responsibility for the choices one makes in all areas of life. In some countries, conservative ideology includes elements of religion, accountability to God, and social hierarchy under God.

Both religious and secular conservatism adopt a generally pessimistic view of human nature. They hold that most people, most of the time, are inclined to do evil. This tendency toward the negative is deemed to be innate. Christians see this negative bent as a consequence of the Adamic fall; political conservatives usually see it simply as a given, as amply demonstrated throughout history. Both perspectives also assume that human nature does not change, even over time.

Both types of conservatism also reject the notion that education will eventually solve most of our moral problems. They believe that the main problem is not that people are uneducated. They point out that some of the most evil people of all times, including many Nazi leaders in Hitler's Germany, were extremely well educated. Indeed, the masses who cheered Hitler wildly were among the most educated people in the world.

Both types of conservatism also reject any belief in natural and inevitable human progress and moral evolution. Instead Christian conservatives and at times also political conservatives claim to discern a distinct decline in public and personal morality.

The notions of hierarchy and authority are popular among both Christian and secular conservatives. Christians place God at the top, with government and other authority centers below him and accountable to him. Families, led by the father, form their own hierarchical structure as the fundamental building block of society. Many political conservatives also lean to this view, although in recent decades, especially with the inroads of feminism, this hierarchical bent is rapidly receding.

Because both groups view the masses as not enlightened

morally, they sometimes harbor some suspicions about democracy and extensive majority rule, whether in the community, at school, at work, or in political jurisdictions. They argue that just as only the truly competent person—not just anybody—should work as a mechanic, a teacher, a physician, or a bridge builder, so also not just anybody, or everybody for that matter, should be in charge in politics. Confidence in the judgment of the masses is weak, especially for Christian conservatives but, at least historically, also for many political conservatives. The exceptions would be those conservatives, Christians and others, who have subscribed to populist notions of faith in the "unspoiled" masses. One is reminded of Alexander Hamilton's famous statement "It is an unquestionable truth that the body of the people in every country do not possess the discernment and stability necessary for systematic government." Not many political conservatives would go that far today.

Both groups tend to see moral issues in black and white, although this is not always expressed or fully embraced, and opponents are seen as not only different but also in error. And it's very hard to feel good about giving equal time and full freedom to error! Both also tend to support some forms of censorship, Sunday closing laws, tax benefits for churches and clergy, a religious element in public education, a virtual ban on abortion, and strong support for traditional marriages and traditional families. Both Christian and political conservatism tend to see compromise on key beliefs—I stress *key beliefs*—not as an acceptance of the happy medium but as an undesirable, although perhaps necessary, yielding of principle.

Both types of conservatism generally, but not always, also identify with the following notions: the best times lie in the past; morally, at least, things are getting worse; and past experience is a good moral reference point. Both also agree that our present way of life is the achievement of many generations of experience and should not be tampered with too readily, that any basic changes should be undertaken slowly and cautiously, that people are not inherently equal, and that law and order deserve strong emphasis.

Many political conservatives emphasize the importance of religion, whether Christianity or some other faith. They assert that religion plays a basic role in the development and maintenance of a good society. A major supposed benefit of a strong religious belief is that fear of punishment by God reduces crime. While political conservatives sometimes focus on the Christian faith or on Judeo-Christian values, they are typically not inclined to emphasize the uniqueness of the Christian gospel. Conservative Christians are widely drawn to such a religious emphasis. However, more than a few observers have argued that for some political conservatives this may be more a means to an end, namely, the achievement of voter support rather than actual endorsement of Christianity or any other faith.

Despite these considerable areas of overlap, the differences between the two types of conservatism are substantial. When true to their creed, conservative Christians are very strong on humanitarian assistance; political conservatives are typically not as enthusiastic about such undertakings. We must note, however, that at times within secular conservatism there is a strong emphasis on what is termed *noblesse oblige,* a moral obligation incumbent upon rich or otherwise privileged people to act generously and honorably toward the less fortunate. In other situations, political conservatives have shown an amazing indifference to the needs and plight of "the lower classes."

Conservative Christianity stands for selflessness and a deep concern for one's neighbors. Political conservatism is more likely to stress individual and national self-centeredness, less concern for the needy and oppressed, and a willingness to accept substantial social and at times even economic inequality. We must not press this contrast too far, however.

Political conservatives who are also Christians will typically bring their social ethic to their political involvement.

Political conservatives make much of property rights; conservative Christians also see value in property rights but not as strongly. After all, Christians are stewards under God and therefore ought to hold their property loosely.

Finally, political conservatives have tended to emphasize patriotism and nationalism; often one's country seems to constitute the highest good. If true to their creed, conservative Christians see matters differently. They give first allegiance to Christ and the Christian church, which is ultimately transnational, and therefore all other allegiances, including patriotism, must be secondary and conditional.

Given the above similarities and even with the areas of important differences, it is not surprising that political conservatism seems to be the most favored political ideology for Christians, especially in prosperous societies.

Socialism

We turn now to an analysis of socialism. The German theologian Paul Tillich once observed, "Christianity is the religion of which socialism is the practice." As we analyze the essentials of socialism, let us assess the validity of his assertion. Should Christians follow the example of the early Jerusalem church and be attracted to socialism, or at least its economic component? By *socialism* I mean the democratic forms as expressed by the Labour Party in the United Kingdom, the New Democratic Party in Canada, and similar parties elsewhere. The undemocratic forms associated with Joseph Stalin or Fidel Castro belong in a separate category. For the past two and a half centuries, democratic socialism has become a significant factor in most western democracies, although in a few, most notably the United States, it has never gained a substantial following.

Democratic socialism is optimistic about human nature; people are seen as inherently good. According to this view, evil in society can be explained by the fact that people have been corrupted by the evils of capitalism. According to this view, the existence of evil is thus the result not of any Adamic fall but of exploitative economic social structures. Accordingly, the way to counteract evil is to get rid of capitalism. Education, it is believed, can be very useful here because it will enable people to understand and to eradicate the evils of capitalist exploitation.

Further, socialism holds that a person is primarily an economic being, that class structure is the dominant feature of industrially mature societies, and that most people identify themselves fundamentally as members of an economic class. It is also argued that people readily cooperate to advance the common good and desire to function collectively. From this perspective, government is the agency of the dominant class, and it rules, mainly, for the benefit of the class it represents. Thus the traditionally capitalist political parties have ruled for the benefit of the capitalist class. Under a socialist regime, the government's task is to restructure society by democratic means so that it can eliminate capitalist exploitation and then proceed to serve the interests of the ordinary working people, presumed to be the most moral class in society. The result will be that all people will be treated well.

Socialists generally argue that government, in which they have very great faith, should not only eliminate exploitation but also establish economic equality to a considerable degree. It should also provide extensive medical and social-welfare programs funded by taxation. Alongside these humanitarian undertakings, the government should—at least ideally—legislate public ownership of the major agencies of production and distribution, such as railways, utilities, mines, banks, and large manufacturing companies. Government should also enact legislation highly favorable to labor unions. A centrally planned economy is also important, at least for some groups of democratic socialists.

Most socialists denounce greed and the personal acquisition of great wealth. They also believe that with correct social engineering, society can be reshaped into something much better than capitalism creates. In that new society, hunger and deprivation will be eliminated. Historically, their slogan was "From each according to his ability; to each according to his need."

Given this description, what are the areas of overlap with Christianity? Both socialism and Christianity express a deep concern to help the needy, the oppressed, and the marginalized. Both want to end economic exploitation and abuse. Both reject greed and seek a fairer distribution of wealth so that all people can escape dire poverty. Both thus support some economic leveling, but socialism takes that notion much further than does Christianity. It moves beyond voluntarism to legislated coercion and that is a major qualitative shift.

An emphasis on community, a rejection of destructive nationalistic rivalries—socialists speak of international classes—and a strong bent toward international cooperation also suggest some Christian values. Similarly, the idea that the economic causes of war should be eliminated resonates with at least part of the Christian concern for peace and "the brotherhood of man."

In reviewing the common agenda, especially concerning injustices stemming from the worst elements in the Industrial Revolution, we do well to remember that many of the most influential socialist reformers, especially in the United Kingdom and Canada, drew heavily on their Christian faith. With considerable justification, it has been said that these socialist reformers owed "as much to Methodism as to Marxism."

Despite significant areas of congruence, the areas of difference are extensive. Conservative Christians cannot agree with the notion that human nature is basically good or that if human nature is evil it is so because capitalism has corrupted it. They do not locate the source of evil in economic exploitation, bad as that may be in many situations, but in the sinful Adamic fall. They believe that sin causes economic exploitation, not that economic exploitation causes sin. The distinction is important. Further, although valuing education, conservative Christians do not consider education to be a major corrective for evil and do not agree that the proper "study of man" should focus largely on economics. They also reject the standard socialist belief that correct teaching and policy will bring about something called "the new socialist man." They look to spiritual regeneration to achieve that goal.

While conservative Christians acknowledge the existence of economic classes, they do not agree with the assumed centrality of class analysis or with the assumed inevitability of class conflict. Indeed they and other observers point out that most people do not identify themselves primarily as members of a class. They remind us that in the great wars of the twentieth century, as in earlier times, the masses of the people placed national identity and nationalistic feelings far ahead of membership in a supposed transnational economic brotherhood.

Additionally, conservative Christians reject the marginalizing of the individual, the widespread discrimination in favor of "the working class," unwarranted faith in big government, and the strong emphasis on central planning and regulation. Socialist justification of virtually all labor strikes is another problem for many conservative Christians.

In short, while there are some important areas of commonality, conservative Christianity and secular socialism explain evil differently, offer different solutions to moral failings, and generally have different ideals and priorities.

Liberalism

We turn now to an analysis of secular liberalism, particularly the more enlightened modern version widely known as reform liberalism. It has moved beyond the classical notion of laissez-faire, the idea that government should largely step back and let the unseen hands of the marketplace take over.

In modern reform liberalism, as in socialism, human nature is viewed as basically good, not evil. The rampant evil found in society is supposedly caused mainly by the fact that people are ignorant and have not been enlightened by education. The responsibility for evil thus lies mainly with society and its institutions, not with the individual. Educational reform and correct government policies are pivotal goals. Liberals argue that correct education will solve most moral problems. For example, where racial hatred exists, bring in more education.

Further, liberals generally hold to an optimistic view of human motivation, namely, that once people come to understand what is in their own interest, they will act accordingly. This is generally a critically important trait of liberalism.

Pointing to the causes of many wars throughout history, liberals refuse to support aggressive or militant nationalism. They also reject notions of ethnic purity and any form of divisive tribalism. Instead they tend to give much support to the idea of "the brotherhood of man."

Liberals look optimistically to the future. Society is evolving. The good times lie ahead. But to expand freedom and increase opportunity, people need governmental initiative and assistance.

While fully committed to both individualism and liberty —the two cardinal values of liberalism—they believe that the government should help every individual to develop his or her potential as fully as possible. Those people who are unable to achieve such development by themselves, for whatever reason, must be helped by the government as well as by volunteers. Significantly, government should not set any ultimate personal goals or values; individuals need to set these for themselves.

Given this description, what are the areas of overlap with

Christianity, particularly conservative Christianity? The emphasis on humanitarianism is common: man is his brother's keeper. The truly needy should be assisted by the more privileged. Similarly, liberalism and conservative Christianity share a concern for some, but not drastic, economic equalization; both refuse to rationalize inequity as mere fate.

A belief in the moral worth of all peoples and of every individual characterizes both Christianity and political liberalism. While the Christian asserts that every person is made in the image of God and therefore possesses dignity, the liberal asserts that every person possesses great potential and that all people are of equal worth. Both strongly reject any Marxist notion of describing people primarily in economic or class terms.

The two views agree on the importance of liberty and of individual choices in the area of faith commitments. They also agree on the desirability of developing a person's potential. For liberals, however, this emphasis is largely directionless; for Christians, it has a specific Christian goal: to live as much as possible by the ethic Jesus taught and modeled.

The two perspectives agree in their rejection of militant nationalism and their emphasis on internationalism. Christians stress the transnational nature of the church of Jesus Christ and of overseas aid, often as part of a missionary endeavor. As we have noted, liberals stress "the brotherhood of man" and secularly motivated international assistance.

Despite these significant areas of congruence, conservative Christianity and political liberalism have major areas of tension and disagreement. Their views of human nature are basically different. Christians root individual and societal evil largely in the Adamic fall. They reject the liberal assumption that ignorance is the cause of evil and education is the remedy.

Especially important, Christians reject the liberal assumption that people can be taught to know their own self-interest and, even more important, that they will act according to their own self-interest once they comprehend it. Christians point out that it is not only little children who choose to eat unhealthy diets and who spend their money foolishly. Nor is it only the children who do not go to the dentist when they know they should. It cannot be assumed, Christians assert, that if adults know what is best—what is in their self-interest—they will do it.

Given that people often consciously choose to do what is not best or not even in their own self-interest, conservative Christians also do not have blind faith in majority rule. Majorities have often been wrong. Consider for example what majorities did to Socrates, Jesus, and Galileo. Insights and wisdom, they observe, do not come to majorities spontaneously. Often it takes a long time for minorities who have come to some important insight or conviction to convince the majority about the merit of the new insight or conviction. The rejection of slavery, the emancipation of women, the rejection of child labor, and the value of public education for both boys and girls were all championed by minorities long before the majorities supported such views.

Conservative Christians also generally reject the widespread liberal faith in big government and in government initiatives. Finally, they also see little basis for liberal optimism or for the assumption that if we use our minds well, the best times lie ahead in terms of moral progress and societal well-being.

Conclusion

These, then, are the typical political worldviews competing for Christian support. As we encounter such overtures, let us make wise choices. In doing so, let us not hitch the cause of Christ to any political party or ideology. The cause of Christ is of a higher order. And let us not misapply Scripture. More than a few Christians, either in jest or seriously, have quoted Ecclesiastes 10:2 as support for their right-wing beliefs: "The heart of the wise inclines to the right, but the heart of the fool to the left." I suggest that the brilliant Solomon did not have the modern left-right political spectrum in mind when he wrote this verse.

As we all face political choices, let us in every situation carefully discern the best option and support it to the extent we deem advisable. If no option merits our support or is appealing, it may still be in our interest to support the lesser evil concerning political parties, elections, and policy options.

11

Is There a Biblical Basis for Civil Disobedience?

A BASIC REQUIREMENT for the functioning of civil society is that citizens obey the law of the land. Christians and most other people agree with this principle. The logic is compelling: if substantial numbers of citizens decided for themselves which laws they would obey and which they would not obey, anarchy would result rather quickly.

Actually, the situation is more complicated than that. What should citizens do if the government introduces laws they cannot obey without violating their conscience and disobeying God? Such a dilemma is not just theoretical. There have been countless situations since biblical times in which such a dilemma existed.

What should Christians do when governments pressure them to violate their conscience? The central idea in this analysis is that, after having done all they can to solve the problem in other ways, Christians have a right to undertake civil disobedience rather than do something that is inherently evil or which their Christian conscience forbids them to do. In many situations, a negotiated solution can be found. For example, some hospitals will transfer nurses to other work areas if they refuse to participate in abortions. Some employers will respect people who refuse to work on Sundays. And some governments will allow alternative service for people who would otherwise be forced to join the military forces.

However, sometimes it is not possible to get the government orders changed or to negotiate exemptions. A dictatorial government will not tolerate any criticism, yet most Christians feel they must speak out against extreme injustice. In such predicaments a carefully calculated and sensitively carried-out form of civil disobedience may be the most moral of reactions.

I must emphasize that in any situation, civil disobedience is always a last resort and is warranted only if all other peaceful options have failed. It should also be stated at the outset that the type of civil disobedience being discussed here is not undertaken to overthrow a government but to get the government to change a particular policy.

The assumption that reasonable people will use their own judgments in determining what is right and what is wrong is actually widespread. We do well to recall that during the Nuremberg war crimes trials after World War II, the victorious Allied leaders prosecuted and punished the Nazi civilian and military leaders not for *disobeying* the laws of the land but for *obeying* Hitler's orders. The prosecutors argued and the courts agreed that enlightened, rational people should have recognized the grave evil in Hitler's legal orders and in the name of decency and a higher moral law should have disobeyed him. The prosecutors argued that they should have practiced civil disobedience and that some deserved the death penalty for not doing so. Many of the accused argued that they were obeying the law of the land and that everything Hitler had done had been legal. The Allied judges rejected that argument and many Nazi leaders were executed for failing to be disobedient.

After World War II, much praise was heaped on certain

groups that did practice civil disobedience. The Dutch family who hid Anne Frank and Norwegian teachers who refused to teach the Nazi curriculum in their classrooms are examples. Praise also went to the Swedish diplomat Raoul Wallenberg, who indulged in civil disobedience by illegally issuing passports to thousands of Hungarian Jews who were otherwise headed for the Nazi gas chambers. These practitioners of civil disobedience became global heroes.

In later years the American civil rights movement led by Martin Luther King Jr. indulged in massive disobedience to achieve fairer treatment for blacks. At first, many condemned this civil disobedience. However, after some years the United States government, in establishing a national holiday to honor him, announced that King's cause had been just and his civil disobedience morally correct.

Civil disobedience also played a major role in ending apartheid in South Africa. In eastern Europe it played a large part in defeating Communism. It also allowed American slaves to escape to Canada more than a century ago. We can also cite biblical accounts, such as baby Moses being hidden in the bulrushes of the Nile River, an illegal act.

It is important to note that in all these instances the motive of those who courageously decided to practice civil disobedience was not personal benefit. Rather their motivations were for truly needy people or to achieve a basic reform that would benefit society as a whole. A higher good and a higher law were invoked.

In our own day, civil disobedience has been practiced in smuggling Bibles into certain countries, in picketing abortion clinics, in assisting refugees, and in assembling for Christian worship when told not to do so. The actual list of situations would be very long.

Many of those who engage in civil disobedience argue that as governments in many lands adopt increasingly anti-Christian policies and as public morality deteriorates,

Christians will increasingly find themselves driven to civil disobedience. A consistent Christian ethic will, they say, leave them no other option. The issue is hotly debated among Christians as well as non-Christians. Be that as it may, for more and more Christians, the issue cannot be avoided.

Definitions

We need to be clear about our definitions. *Civil disobedience* refers to a public, nonviolent act contrary to law, undertaken for reason of conscience. The intent is to draw attention to evil and to have the situation changed. Generally, the object is to help others, not oneself. At times, however, the issue does involve only oneself or a small group.

Closely related to civil disobedience is *conscientious objection,* the refusal to undertake something demanded by government that violates one's conscience. In this practice, one does not so much want to change a law or policy as to be exempted from it. Examples include refusing to register for military conscription, refusing to serve on a jury, and refusing to present children for vaccination.

A category of civil disobedience that differs from the usual type is sometimes called *tactical civil disobedience.* Here the intent is not so much to get rid of a law as to test its meaning or constitutionality. King often used this tactic to show that various laws were never intended to suppress black people or that they were inherently unconstitutional. This tactic usually results in a court case that settles an issue or at least points to its resolution.

We should also distinguish between *direct civil disobedience* and *indirect civil disobedience.* By direct civil disobedience we mean some act that addresses a problem directly. An example would be a group of blacks who, in an effort to end racial segregation, sit at a lunch counter reserved for whites. Conversely, when a group of people illegally blocks highway traffic in an attempt to draw attention to someone who's been imprisoned illegally, that is called *indirect* civil disobedience. These people are not opposed to the traffic; they are opposed to something else and want that injustice publicized. They want to inform people about their friend in prison and to motivate strangers to help them correct the supposed injustice.

Does the Bible say anything about civil disobedience? Although it teaches that governments are ordained by God and that all citizens, including Christians, should generally obey governments, we do find texts that address this topic.

We have already referred to the account given in Exodus 2:1-9, in which Moses' life was illegally spared. As we read in Exodus 1:15-22, the civil disobedience of certain Jewish midwives was quite widespread. These midwives "feared God, and did not do as the king of Egypt had told them to do. . . . So God was kind to the midwives." Clearly, God was pleased by their civil disobedience and rewarded them.

It can be argued that the Old Testament justification for civil disobedience as a tactic derives from the exhortation of Deuteronomy 6:5: "Love the Lord your God with all your heart and with all your soul and with all your strength." Jesus repeats this command of unconditional allegiance in Matthew 22:37 and Mark 12:30. Many other biblical passages also instruct true believers to worship only God.

The book of Daniel provides two examples of civil disobedience that pleased God. The first involved the refusal of Shadrach, Meshach, and Abednego to obey King Nebuchadnezzar's command to worship the golden image (see Daniel 3:18). The second involved Daniel's refusal to pray only to King Darius (see Daniel 6).

In the New Testament we find numerous examples of praiseworthy law breaking. The picking of some grain and the healing by Jesus on the Sabbath could be cited as cases in point. In Mathew 12:1-13, Jesus declared that he was Lord of the Sabbath. In Matthew 2:1-12, we read how the Magi, warned by God in a dream, disobeyed Herod's command that they report to him after completing their visit to the infant Jesus. It is important to note that God instructed them to disobey the king and indulge in civil disobedience; here we have direct civil disobedience specifically commanded by God.

Some Christians object to any justification of civil disobedience and cite Romans 13:1 to support this stance. The verse says, "Everyone must submit himself to the governing authorities, for there is no authority except that which God has established." Two responses must be carefully considered. First, the issue in this passage is being subject to the institution of government, not obeying every conceivable order issued by a government. Paul was telling the Roman Christians that they should accept the legitimacy of the political authorities instead of submitting to God only and thus supporting some sort of political anarchy. Second, the fact that Paul's stance did not mean unconditional obedience to all government directives is clear from his own life. He continued to preach even after the authorities flogged him, imprisoned him, and ordered him to stop.

The other apostles also continued preaching under similar conditions. Note their response when commanded not to preach: "But Peter and John replied, 'Judge for yourselves whether it is right in God's sight to obey you rather than God. For we cannot help speaking about what we have seen and heard'" (Acts 4:19-20). Later the civic-religious authorities in the Sanhedrin instructed them a second time, "We gave you strict order not to teach in this name." But they could not bring an end to the civil disobedience, for "Peter and the other apostles replied: 'We must obey God rather than men!'" (Acts 5:28- 29).

We need to reemphasize that the purpose of civil disobedience is to convince authorities that a law, regulation, policy, or practice is inherently wrong. Then the authorities will, it is hoped, accede by their own free will to the moral request of those practicing the civil disobedience. Typically, the purpose in bringing about the change is not to seek any personal gain but to achieve justice for a group or a fundamental reform for society as a whole. Sometimes, however, as with the preaching apostles, the main issue may not be the desire to get a law changed but a continuing willingness to practice civil disobedience if obedience to God requires such action.

Secular Arguments for Civil Disobedience

Most of the authors of literature justifying civil disobedience argue mainly on secular grounds. In his classic work *On the Duty of Civil Disobedience,* Henry David Thoreau wrote, "We should be men first, and subjects afterward. It is not desirable to cultivate respect for the law, so much as for the right." Seventeenth-century English philosopher and theologian John Locke wrote that citizens are free moral agents and have "rights against the state." He asserted that citizens have a right to disobey and even to rebel when rulers grossly violate or neglect the purposes for which government was established. Rebellion, however, lies outside of the category of civil disobedience.

In the early twentieth century, Thomas Hill Green wrote that it is the function of government to maintain "those conditions of freedom which are the conditions of the moral life. . . . If it ceases to serve this function, it loses its claim on our obedience." Another modern writer, John Rawls, points out that often the truly moral person faces two options: either undertake civil disobedience or become a party to the evil being perpetrated. Like other writers, he argues that, from the times Socrates and Jesus down to the modern-day horrors of Nazism and apartheid, history has amply demonstrated that majorities are often wrong and that individuals and small groups must practice civil disobedience to bring about moral improvement.

Virtually all defenders of civil disobedience as a basic right, and at times even as a duty, stress that a person should take this step as a last resort, only after all other peaceful and legal options have been exhausted. Of course, sometimes, as in rigid dictatorships, other peaceful and legal means may not be available.

For Christians there is one other basic consideration. Our commitment to God is primary and all other claims are subordinate. If the orders of an authority contradict the orders of God, they must be disobeyed. In matters of faith and morality, what Christians believe and do can never be dictated by the rulers of the day. For a Christian, disobedience to God is always more serious than disobedience to the state.

Some Christians believe that civil disobedience is appropriate for only certain kinds of issues. Concerning the right to worship God, to serve him, to preach the gospel, and to undertake evangelism, these Christians say they have a right to practice civil disobedience if all else fails. But they draw the line at Christians practicing civil disobedience on behalf of other causes, even when injustice, oppression, and torture are at stake.

Others argue that when these other great evils, those not related to Christian activity, exist, Christians have a duty to undertake civil disobedience for themselves and especially for others. They assert that Christians who truly want to uphold what is right may have "to become the enemy of a state which has made itself the enemy of the people."[1]

Some Christian supporters of a broad view of the need, or even duty, to practice civil disobedience stress that it is always best to check matters with a larger Christian community. They argue that there is wisdom in numbers. Some also point out that, whether acting as individuals or groups, Christians need to acknowledge that even a conscience informed by Christian commitment may be in error. It may misjudge a situation and may not be hearing the true voice of

God. Consequently, caution and very careful analysis of a situation are always in order.

Objections to Civil Disobedience

In deciding if civil disobedience is appropriate in any situation, all citizens, but especially Christians, ought to take note of the major criticisms of civil disobedience. These objections deserve careful consideration.

1. **Civil disobedience undermines law and order.** This may seem to be the case, but the situation is more complicated than that. Despotic governments often cloak tyranny and oppression in the language of legal action. The official sanctioning of apartheid, infanticide, the Holocaust, and restrictions on religious freedom are not made more acceptable by being made legal, not even with majority support. Martin Luther King Jr. said, "We should never forget that everything that Adolf Hitler did in Germany was legal." We also recall St. Augustine's statement "An unjust law is no law at all."

   I must emphasize the point that civil disobedience, especially when rooted in Christian teaching, does not challenge the need for government or its mandate to make laws. In this sense it differs fundamentally from the stance of anarchism, which opposes the institution of government itself. Another statement by King underscores the point: "I submit that an individual who breaks a law that conscience tells him is unjust, and willingly accepts the penalty by staying in jail to arouse the conscience of the community over its injustice is, in reality, expressing the highest respect for the law." Henry David Thoreau's observation is equally timely: "They are the lovers of the law who observe the law when the government breaks it."

2. **If civil disobedience were practiced by many people, it would negate the conditions under which it is possible.** In other words, without majority acceptance of the law, there can be no peaceful and selective rejection of a specific law. The response to this objection is that civil disobedience never involves rejection of all laws, only rejection of a specific law. Support for all other laws continues. Even if there were massive rejection of a set of laws, let's say of Hitler's Holocaust laws, in the name of justice and human dignity, the outcome would not be political instability. Rather it would be an improved society.

3. **The practice of even the most responsible civil disobedience by Christians runs the risk of being misunderstood and thereby weakening the church's larger evangelical mandate.** This is an important but not a determining objection. Christians constantly run the risk of being misunderstood. Those who practice civil disobedience have an obligation to do their best to demonstrate the differences among the rioter, the self-serving dissenter, the publicity seeker, the anarchist, and the selfless moralist who seeks the good of others. In any event, for Christians it is more important to do what is right than to be judged as doing something erroneously perceived to be wrong.

Justifying Civil Disobedience

The question may be asked, "Given all these factors, when is civil disobedience actually justified?" As I see it, it is justified when the following seven conditions are met:

1. The situation must be truly serious. Most situations in which a law is disliked do not warrant the use of civil disobedience. The situation must involve an egregious evil.

2. Great moral seriousness must be demonstrated on the part of those who plan to practice civil disobedience. They

must explain why they are planning to act as they do and must take personal responsibility for their actions. They are not cowards; they do not run and hide.

3. The specific goal must be clearly identified and must be shown to be of benefit to many people or even to the entire community.

4. All legal means of correcting the evil must already have been exhausted.

5. Before, during, and after an act of civil disobedience, basic respect for law and order must be affirmed and practiced.

6. Only suitable means should be used. The means must never undermine the ends.

7. Punishment must be accepted without resistance. The person practicing civil disobedience readily admits legal guilt, albeit within a larger explanation of moral innocence according to a higher law. The willing acceptance of morally unwarranted punishment greatly enhances the morality of the law-breaking event.

Conclusion

While in advanced democracies the need for civil disobedience may be rare, the need does occur. In some other countries, where laws and practices are often unjust, the need may arise more frequently.

A readiness to undertake civil disobedience constitutes a part of giving unqualified primary allegiance to God. Breaking the law of the land is always serious but it is not always wrong, as even the biblical examples have shown.

Perhaps the most controversial aspect of civil disobedience involves determining the kinds of situations in which it is justified. Undertaking it as Daniel did by worshipping God has gained broad support among Christians. Similarly, undertaking it as the apostles did by proclaiming the gospel as described in Acts has also been widely affirmed. But to undertake it on behalf of social causes relating to racism, the environment, unfair labor legislation, and similar concerns is less widely supported. What some see as self-evident, given Jesus' emphasis on loving one's neighbor, others see as unjustified. This debate must continue, and it must be continued in an atmosphere of mutual respect.

12

How Should Christians
Pray for Politicians
and Governments?

WHILE THE BIBLE contains numerous statements about how Christians should relate to governmental authorities, and while government institutions are strongly affirmed by Jesus and other biblical teachers, relatively little is said in Scripture about the place of political matters in a believer's prayer life. In the Old Testament we find some statements dealing with prayer and political matters, but these are generally focused on cities or countries, not on officials. Perhaps the best known of these is found in Psalm 122:6, where we read that we are to "pray for the peace of Jerusalem." We also find instances of rulers themselves praying for what we might call political well-being. For example, in 1 Chronicles 21:17 David confessed his sin to God and interceded for his people. Hezekiah prayed for deliverance from Sennacherib (see 2 Kings 19:19). Mordecai and his Jewish associates prayed and fasted when Queen Esther was involved in heavy discussions with King Xerxes for the safety of others (see Esther 4:12-17).

A clear command to pray for specific rulers is found in

Ezra 6:10: "Pray for the well-being of the king and his sons."
That our prayers for politicians should extend even to those
rulers who are evil is evident from Matthew 5:44, in which
Jesus commands, "Pray for those who persecute you," and in
Luke 6:28, in which he says, "Pray for those who mistreat
you."

The command to pray for even ungodly rulers is in line
with God's statement to the non-believing King Cyrus when he
said, "For the sake of Jacob my servant, of Israel my chosen, I
will call you by name and bestow on you a title of honor,
though you do not acknowledge me. . . . I will strengthen you,
though you have not acknowledged me" (Isaiah 45:4-5). If
God sees fit to honor and empower ungodly rulers, Christians
should certainly be willing to pray for them.

In the New Testament, various passages exhort believers
to obey, pay taxes to, and be thankful for their governments.
But we have only one specific command to pray for governments. Paul's command in 1 Timothy 2:1-3 provides clear
guidelines.

> I urge, then, first of all, that requests, prayers, interces-
> sion and thanksgiving be made for everyone—for kings
> and all those in authority, that we may live peaceful and
> quiet lives in all holiness.
> This is good, and pleases God our Savior.

Of course, we also have a general biblical mandate to
pray for people according to their needs. And we are instructed to proclaim the good news to all and to invite all people
to accept salvation and the lordship of Christ. We do not
have a model prayer concerning intercession for governments, and the Lord's Prayer found in Matthew 6 makes no
reference to political authorities. Nonetheless we have sufficient instruction in this area to develop some guidelines and
suggestions.

How Should We Pray for Governments?

What specific items relating to government should be on our prayer lists? While some of the specifics will vary from one country and situation to another, the following list is a useful starting point. As a set of goals, it should be periodically reviewed and updated. Naturally, not all items will be applicable at all times.

1. **We should pray that rulers practice personal integrity.** The peaceful functioning of government requires public trust and confidence. If rulers are seen to be dishonest and lacking in personal morality, the fragile fabric of a stable and peaceful society may be weakened or even unravel. By setting a bad example, dishonest rulers send a message that it is acceptable to lie, steal, cheat, and so on, a lesson easily learned by others, especially the younger folk. They should not be surprised if citizens then do likewise. Honest tax collection, law enforcement, and the general maintenance of law and order become very difficult if rulers are evil and if they live by a "do as I say, not as I do" axiom.

   The importance of personal integrity on the part of our rulers also extends to areas such as sexual behavior, treatment of spouse and children, and a commitment to what has been promised in election campaigns. Many a ruler has fallen from grace or even lost his or her office, because of lack of integrity in these matters.

2. **We should pray that rulers will make wise decisions and rule justly.** For rulers, as for others, wisdom has two components: knowing the truth and acting on the truth. Many people, rulers and others, who know the truth and know what should be done are not willing to do what is right. Throughout Scripture, God calls rulers to pursue wisdom and justice.

Our rulers are extremely busy people. The demands on their time are almost unbelievable. They have little time to sit back and reflect. We ought to pray that they will take time to assess what they are doing, that they will be committed to rule justly, and that they will have the courage to do what they know is just.

3. **We should pray that governments will do good for their citizens.** Romans 13:4 is very emphatic: a ruler "is God's servant to do you good." Doing good can take many forms, depending on the most urgent needs of the population. It may involve listening to grievances and trying to address them appropriately, helping the needy, providing essential services, and providing security and protection. The list of possibilities is long. The thrust of our prayers in this area should be that governments will correctly identify the good they should do and then be committed to doing it.

4. **We should pray that governments will restrain evil and be moral in punishing evildoers.** Romans 13 reminds us that the punishment of evildoers is a basic function of government. This truth is underscored in 1 Peter 2:13-14: "Submit yourselves for the Lord's sake to every authority instituted among men: whether to the king, as the supreme authority, or to governors, who are sent by him to punish those who do wrong and to commend those who do right." We are instructed here that rightful punishment for evil deeds is a responsibility of government at all levels.

In carrying out this function, governments unfortunately often make huge mistakes. Punishment is sometimes arbitrary and sometimes out of line with the evil being punished. Sometimes torture is used, an activity that is never justified. When governments are careless about who is to be punished, the innocent suffer. The courts play a crucial role here, so we should pray for judges and magistrates.

Miscarriage of justice is truly reprehensible and displeases God. When miscarriage involves the death penalty, the outcome is truly tragic.

While we should pray that our rulers, judges and magistrates will restrain evil and punish wrongdoers, we should also pray that they will address the causes of crime and employ redemptive policies whenever possible. In an increasing number of countries, offenders, especially youthful ones, are being steered away from a life of crime by positive initiatives like reconciliation programs and sentences that involve restitution or community service.

Christians especially should be looking for enlightened ways of addressing evil and dealing with evildoers. Evil cannot be ignored. It must be punished, but there are often better options than imprisonment. We should pray that governments will pursue and implement such options.

5. **We should pray that those who govern us will have the health and strength to carry out their God-given tasks.** While our governmental leaders may be exalted in human terms, they are mere human beings with typical frailties, weaknesses, and illnesses. They have awesome responsibilities and they need good health and strength. It is right that we pray for them in this regard and also that we pray for their protection. They are, after all, servants and agents of God.

6. **We should pray that our rulers will pursue ways of peace.** Those who rule can be easily tempted to undertake unwarranted military action. After all, in most cases a war tends to unite the population, produce greater support for the government, and generate an economic upsurge, at least in the short run. Rulers are therefore sometimes tempted to provoke an international crisis and thus precipitate war.

Of course, wars occur for other reasons as well. They can result because of a desire of a government to right a presumed earlier wrong, because of a border dispute, because of a desire to enlarge the boundaries of a country or an empire, because of a desire to seek economic advantage, or simply to indulge in revenge. The long-term consequences are almost always disastrous. Christians should pray that governments avoid wars, and if a war begins, that it will cease. All Christians should pray that the ethnic, religious, tribal, or regional tensions will be healed and that those in authority seriously seek ways of dealing peacefully with such tensions.

7. **We should pray that our governments will manage the economy carefully and wisely.** We should ask God to grant them wisdom as they develop policies in economic matters ranging from taxation to currency management, from trade negotiations to planning, and from budgeting to debt reduction. This, too, is part of the divine mandate to "do good." Unwise planning, reckless spending, irresponsible deficit financing, and runaway inflation have brought untold grief to millions of people. It is in the interest of all people, including Christians, that rulers not undermine economic stability and development.

8. **We should pray that God will guide our rulers as they establish priorities.** One of the toughest duties of governments is to decide which problems are in most urgent need of attention. Problems relating to healthcare, education, food supply, road construction, housing, helping the destitute, and many other urgent matters all clamor for attention. Governments never have sufficient resources to do everything that needs to be done and need our prayers in this area.

9. **We should pray that our rulers will encourage a climate of freedom,** especially freedom of speech and freedom of religion. Governments are constantly tempted to restrict freedom in order to exercise control and promote particular agendas. We should pray that, other than in times of great emergency, they will not restrict basic freedoms. And we pray that even in times of emergency, freedoms will not be restricted any more than absolutely necessary.

10. **We should pray that our governments will defend and uphold human dignity.** It is a basic quality of good government that much emphasis is placed on human dignity. This emphasis should impact all people but especially the elderly, the infirm, the destitute, refugees, and those in prison. Some Christians would argue that those not yet born should be put at the head of the list. Because we stress that all people are made in the image of God and have a spark of the divine within them, Christian citizens are particularly committed to upholding human dignity.

11. **We should pray that governments will work govern for the common good,** not for their own advantage and not for the advantage of a small group of elites who would benefit at the expense of the masses.

12. **We should pray that governments will be open to good counsel and advice, including that from Christians.** No government has a corner on understanding and insight, and all rulers should be willing to listen to the constructive criticism and policy suggestions of others.

13. **We should pray that our rulers understand God's role in human affairs and acknowledge their own accountability to God.** Even the ungodly King Nebuchadnezzar came to such an understanding and said so at least twice. After he

had sentenced the three Jewish men to be burned in the fiery furnace and then observed their divine rescue, he proclaimed, "Praise be to the God of Shadrach, Meshach and Abednego, who has sent his angel and rescued his servants" (Daniel 3:28). Later, after his own seven-year punishment to live like an animal, he said, "I, Nebuchadnezzar, praise and exalt and glorify the King of heaven, because everything he does is right and all his ways are just. And those who walk in pride he is able to humble" (Daniel 4:37). Nebuchadnezzar spoke from experience. The once-proud king had learned his lesson; he had come to acknowledge the King of kings.

Let us pray that our own kings and rulers do likewise. They need to understand that God is Lord of all, that God sometimes uses governments as instruments of his power, and that all rulers will someday have to give account to him. They need to acknowledge that "by him all things were created: things in heaven and on earth, visible and invisible, whether thrones or powers or rulers or authorities; all things were created by him and for him" (Colossians 1:16).

14. **We should pray prayers of gratitude for the institution of government.** God has established it for the benefit of his human creatures. He has arranged for us to enjoy the benefits of a society of law and order instead of suffering in anarchy. Even in those situations when we cannot thank God for the political officeholders of the day, we can still thank him for the institution of human government. Perhaps that is what the apostle Paul had in mind when he urged believers to be thankful for the benefits of government (see 1 Timothy 2). Incompetent or evil officeholders will eventually be replaced, but the institution of government will continue. For that fact we should pray prayers of gratitude.

15. Finally, if our rulers are not Christians, we should pray for their salvation. The highest political, social, or economic status here on earth does not benefit anyone in the life to come. All people are in need of salvation and eternal life through Jesus Christ our Lord. The apostle Paul's own action serves as a good example for us. Although he was under arrest, he still challenged King Agrippa to become a Christian. The last word we have is that the king did not respond positively but was almost persuaded. Paul has left us a good example of witnessing to rulers and we should do likewise. It might even happen that rulers are eager to hear the truth. We read, for example, that Sergius Paulus, "the proconsul, an intelligent man, sent for Barnabas and Saul because he wanted to hear the word of God" (Acts 13:7).

Conclusion

At this point the question may be asked, "How can I pray for the well-being of a government that I oppose, despise, and am trying to defeat?" This is an important question. Many Christians find themselves in such situations. Even in difficult realities, however, most of the fifteen principles spelled out above still apply. In fact, some have even greater relevance when the rulers are not good or godly. The important point to keep in mind is that it is ethically consistent to pray that rulers will do what is right, even if we also pray that they will be replaced.

If we are committed to the biblical call to pray for those in authority and if we ask God for insight and guidance in such prayers, he will surely help us to pray intelligently and effectively for those who rule over us.

Conclusion

IF THIS BOOK has one overarching theme it is that Christians need to have an informed and balanced view of politics and government. It argues that, given biblical directives and today's political realities, some of us probably need to revise our assessment of the political order and our view of political structures. In many cases we need to reexamine our thoughts on the government of the day and the officeholders who have the temporary responsibility for it. The officials who have been entrusted by God and by voters to operate the levers of political power deserve nothing less than a balanced assessment and an enlightened response. We need to avoid both unwarranted criticism and cynicism as well as unjustified approval and optimism.

For some—I stress some—readers in the Quaker, Mennonite, and some other traditions, the challenge is to see government, despite its lower ethic, not as the enemy of the church but as a parallel, albeit secondary, agency established by God. More than a few people, Christian and non-Christian, have difficulty viewing government as another demonstration of God's love, an expression of his incredible compassion and concern extended to all people but especially to those who reject his direct lordship.

For other readers the challenge is to reject, or at least revise, a parochial understanding of their own national government as a God-ordained agency alongside the Christian church. The danger is that this association of the two agencies will be drawn too closely. Attempts to fuse God's church with a political cause, either the agenda of a political party or the well-being of an entire country, has been undertaken in many lands. Emperors Constantine and Theodosius I pioneered such efforts in the fourth century. Throughout the Middle Ages and the early modern era, numerous theorists and political leaders tried to fuse God's cause with various political causes. In recent centuries major groups and political parties undertook such efforts in Russia, Germany, Italy, France, the United States, Israel, and many other countries.

The best-known and the most recent major ventures of this type fall into two main categories. One category consists of non-Christian faith groups, such as orthodox Muslim undertakings to fuse religion and national politics and make Allah a tribal deity. Such a stance is found in numerous countries ranging from Iran to Saudi Arabia. In a few other countries, Hindu and Buddhist groups have similarly fused religion and politics.

The second category includes efforts to fuse Christianity with the ideology and program of a political party or the cause of an entire country. This Christian nationalism, as it's been called, has appeared in many countries, but Christian-Americanism is likely the most well-known. In my files I have numerous examples of this reality; some illustrations will make the point.

In the 1960s a movie called *God's Country* drew large audiences. The promotional literature described it thus: "*God's Country* is another feature length, color motion picture epic featuring Tony and Kerry Fontaine. This production is a patriotic presentation of our great American Christian heritage, plus the star spangled message of eternal faith and freedom found only in Jesus Christ." Obviously, such a fusion is cultic. The American flag is not the Christian cross and the pledge of allegiance is not part of the Christian creed. In resisting the domestication of God, Christian citizens in all lands must be careful not to confuse God's favor with God's favoritism and must not allow legitimate patriotism to become idolatry. Fortunately and wisely, the sponsoring company took the controversial film off the market about a decade later.

Even in recent decades, we encounter such thinking. After endorsing Christian-Americanism, the evangelist Billy Graham reversed his stance and wrote, "There have been times in the past when I have, I suppose, confused the kingdom of God with the American way of life. . . . But the kingdom of God is not the same as America."[1] In 1985 Jack Kemp, a U.S. congressman from New York, asserted at a convention of the American Coalition for Traditional Values that "God was the author" of the American Declaration of Independence.[2] The inclination or temptation to fuse God's cause with a nation's cause has a long tradition and can be found in many lands.

While a major thrust of this book is to get people to view politics in a relatively positive light, it also warns believers not to try to make God a Russian, a German, an American, an Italian, a Canadian, an Arab, an Iranian, or any other nationality. Similarly, we should also not try to define God as a socialist, a nationalist, a militarist, a conservative, a liberal, a Democrat, or a Republican. Nor should God be claimed as a mascot for any ideology, party, or country. From Old Testament times to the present, God has worked with and used a great diversity of individual leaders, governments, and countries to achieve his ends. But he is always beyond them and his kingdom is always transnational.

A second overarching issue in this book involves the importance of politics, especially for committed Christians. Some readers may still be asking the basic question, "Why should we take politics seriously?" Some say that politics is part of a sinful and fallen world and that Christians have a more compelling agenda than to get involved in anything related to politics. Such people deserve an answer, one that summarizes much of what has been presented in the previous chapters.

Why Should Christians Take Politics Seriously?

First, Christians should take politics seriously because of the growth of government. In virtually all countries around the world, government has become a massive enterprise. In many lands, all levels of government combined now tax or otherwise collect about half of all income earned by the total population. That's ominous and very consequential. A century ago a common percentage was five to ten percent. Further, today governments have enacted such a vast array of laws and regulations that all of us are impacted all the time.

There are both good and bad consequences of such an invasion into personal lives and into the functioning of society. But the point here is that the impact is great and cannot be ignored. In many countries, government agencies and departments now employ one out of every six or seven working people, and the proportion seems to be increasing. Given these realities, it is hardly surprising that some pundits have said that in many countries, government has replaced the church as the overarching institution within which all other allegiances, agencies, and causes find their place.

Second, Christians should take politics seriously because many governments in many countries now do much of what the church pioneered and much of what the church used to do. This ranges from education at all levels to many forms of healthcare, from assistance for the poor to support for the elderly and the disabled. Since churches and para-church agencies still carry on many of these activities, there is clearly considerable room for cooperation and joint ventures. In some lands, such joint activity can happen easily and the possibilities are extensive. In some other lands, such cooperation is more problematic, either because of specific policies of certain governments or because of their oppressive and exploitative nature.

Third, Christians should take politics seriously because the political arena can be an opportunity for service and ministry. From the local level to the national, there is much Christians can contribute. Good employees—diligent, honest, committed, and dependable—are in demand. And whatever one's view of government, there is much that employees can do without compromising basic ethics. To take the matter a step further, in many government positions, employees and even management staff members have opportunities to practice Christian virtues, such as sensitivity, compassion, other-centeredness, and love. In this connection we may be well advised to give voice to a traditional Guatemalan prayer: "Lord, give bread to those who are hungry, and a hunger for justice to those who have bread."

Opportunities for Christian service are substantial. In fact, because of the need for enlightened decision making and general ethical input, political involvement is one of the most challenging arenas of Christian witnessing. Unfortunately, it also remains one of the most neglected in two respects: on the one hand, because many people shy away from anything termed political, and on the other hand, because some of the Christians in political office separate their personal ethics from what they do on the job.

There are many ways in which a Christian presence will influence what happens in the political arena. These include participation in political party activities, holding elected offices up to a point, working in civil service positions, undertaking legitimate lobbying, submitting views, suggestions, and critiques, and practicing intercessory prayer, a specific directive given to Jesus' followers. As we all consider what we can and should do, the following adage seems to apply: Ability plus opportunity creates responsibility.

Fourth, Christians should take politics seriously because

they have something to say to politicians and governments. We need to inform our leaders that they are the objects of Christians' prayers. When the situation warrants, we need to express affirmation. We need to remember that the input of good people can make government and policies better. History is filled with examples, from Esther in Old Testament times to the anti-smoking lobby in our own day. We need to remind ourselves that the forces of evil will be more effective if other voices remain silent.

The whole structure of government, quite apart from specific reform policies, needs support. Given the ethical malaise typical in a fallen society, we need to acknowledge that stable government is fragile and that democratic government is even more fragile. Given that Scripture as well as experience and reason warn us against anarchy, we do what we can to support the God-ordained institution of government and we do so even when we seek to replace the current officeholders. If we can also in good conscience support the current officeholders, so much the better.

At times people of God also need to express criticism, keeping in mind that we should affirm when we can so that we can with credibility criticize when we must. Richard John Neuhaus makes a valid point when he states, "Democracy and the dissent essential to democracy are mandated by biblical faith."[3] Given the governmental propensity to expand its power and control, enlightened citizens need to challenge authorities. As Neuhaus notes, "Democracy cannot survive without . . . a limiting challenge to the imperiousness of the political."[4]

Despite all of the above, I can still hear some people object. They argue that our message to a fallen world should be a call to repentance. They are right, but only partly. The Old Testament prophets, Jesus and the apostles, and all the New Testament writers also lived in a fallen world. In fact, most lived under very brutal dictatorships. But they all had clear advice and at times even hard-hitting criticism for people who exercised authority. Deciding not to do or say anything in the face of blatant evil, especially if there is opportunity to provide a response, is not particularly praiseworthy and might be called a sin of omission. As I see it, that is not the best time to be "the quiet in the land." The apostle Paul witnessed before King Agrippa in Jerusalem. So also serious Christians in our day should not hesitate to urge rulers to practice justice while also challenging these same authorities to accept salvation and the lordship of Christ.

Christians call all people to respond positively to the gospel, but following Paul's example, we also have other messages for nonbelievers, including secular governments and officeholders. Just as we have a responsibility to try to keep a drunken person from driving, a responsibility to tell people not to steal, and a responsibility to try to prevent cruelty, we likewise have a responsibility to tell authorities to practice justice. That's what the prophets did. We have a responsibility to tell authorities to use no more force than necessary. That's what John the Baptist did. We have a biblical mandate to promote both peace and peacemaking. That's what Jesus stressed in the Sermon on the Mount. We have a responsibility to urge governments not to desecrate the environment. It is God's creation. We have a responsibility to press for decent treatment of marginalized individuals and groups. That's what Jesus taught in Matthew 25. And as we have seen, we have a responsibility to remind even non-Christian rulers that they, like Belshazzar of old, are accountable to God.

Fifth, Christians need to take politics seriously because God does. We need to remember what was and is important to God. If the existence and well-being of civil government as a means of preventing anarchy, thwarting evil, and upholding justice is important to God, as many biblical statements tell us, should it not also be important to us? Since God established the political order with the "mark of Cain," or at whatever other point we think that he did so, should God's people not be committed to its well-being?

Sixth, and perhaps most important, Christians should take politics seriously because of the clear and specific biblical instruction already cited. Followers of the Christian Way have been instructed, not merely advised, to be thankful for the institutions of government and to pray for, honor, and obey governments unless the demands for obedience conflict with God's requirements. We ignore these clear biblical commandments at our peril.

Over the years I have encountered many people who seem very uncomfortable when I refer to governments as agents of God. Some even squirm! But why do they react that way? Don't they read the relevant passages? Don't they believe the Scriptures? Romans 13 is unambiguous; it speaks of the "governing authorities," which "have been established by God" and which "God has instituted." The person who exercises governmental power "is God's servant" and "God's agent." Other passages make similar assertions. Where is there any ambiguity? Where is there room for choice?

Two Kingdoms

At times I have been accused of supporting dualism, a two-kingdom perspective. I readily acknowledge that this is the case. Readers should consider and carefully weigh the following analysis.

God created only one ethic as the right one, but when he gave human beings free choice to accept or reject it, the basis for two groups of people, two ethics, and two ways of life was established. God did not create the two realms or kingdoms, but he gave free choice to his human creation, and that made it possible and perhaps even inevitable.

Jesus referred to this duality of kingdoms many times but perhaps nowhere more explicitly than when he asserted, "My kingdom is not of this world. If it were, my servants would fight to prevent my arrest by the Jews. But now my kingdom is from another place" (John 18:36). By describing the situation as he did, Jesus also explained that there is a different, lower, operational ethic at work among those who reject God's higher ethic.

Acknowledging the lower ethic, an ethic typically operational in the political order, various observers have asked the question, "Can a Christian be involved in politics without affirming that lower ethic?" A related question frequently asked is, "If Christians are involved politically, are they then also responsible for what governments do?" The questions are valid.

The answer to the first is that Christians can be involved at the various levels of government to a considerable extent without affirming the lower ethic typically practiced at that level. Of course, it makes a huge difference if a Christian is a meter reader or mail carrier, or the country's prime minister or president. In such senior positions, indeed in various senior roles, it is extremely difficult for Christians to hold firm to their Christian ethics while also carrying out decisions made by political leaders or even mandated by citizens. Only if their dissent is accepted and respected could they carry on. If Christians hold to pacifist convictions, such high-level involvement is likely impossible.

To a large degree, however, political involvement does not require compromise on essentials, especially in a democracy at lower levels of activity. Where that is a problem, Christians necessarily withdraw. And for those Christians who conclude that they cannot otherwise become involved, they can still pray for those who do decide they can become involved and, of course, for government itself. This is another clear biblical directive.

Those of us who, given our understanding of Scripture, believe that substantive political involvement is compatible with faithful Christian discipleship need to remind ourselves that not all Christians understand the biblical teaching as we do. Given the Christian emphasis on choice and the basic legitimacy of differing views, we all need to respect one another in these matters. Those who read the inspired word differently and then live according to their convictions also convey an important message of living in faithfulness to their understanding of God's expectations in the political realm.

The answer to the question about personal responsibility is also less complicated than one might think. Religious leaders once asked Jesus, "Is it right to pay taxes to Caesar or not?" Jesus and his questioners all knew that Caesar used tax revenues for some very unworthy purposes. Even so, Jesus stated his position clearly: "Give to Caesar what is Caesar's, and to God what is God's" (Matthew 22:17-21). Given this clear teaching by the founder of our faith I have no choice other than to conclude that righteous citizens should pay their taxes and, as situations permit, try to influence the government's allocation and use of its revenues. But they are ultimately not responsible for governmental decisions.

Finally, let me underscore two points. First, in this age of grace and free choice, an age in which most people make many ungodly choices, there will always be tensions between the kingdom of God and the political kingdoms of this world. That is the nature of the situation. We must simply learn to live with such tensions. We do this, in part, by emphasizing the center of the Christian witness, not its boundaries. We also do what we can to resist or roll back the inroads of evil. Do what we can—that is all for which we will ultimately be held accountable. Thomas Moore advised, "When you can't make the good happen, prevent the worst from happening." I am reminded also of Theodore Roosevelt's sage comment, "Do what you can, with what you have, where you are." Second, and most important, if the existence and well-being of governments as a means of preventing anarchy, thwarting evil, and upholding justice is important to God, as the Bible states, should it not also be important to his disciples?

Appendix

160 Selected Biblical Statements on Government and Politics

IT HAS OFTEN BEEN SAID that the Bible has little to say about politics and government and that therefore Christians lack guidance concerning their attitudes and actions in this area. However, a careful reading of the text reveals that even in the mostly dictatorial settings in which the various biblical books were written, a great deal is said about how governments should function, what God expects of political leaders, what God expects of citizens, especially Christian citizens, and how Christians should pray for rulers.

We also read of many godly leaders serving in political offices and using their authority and power to promote justice, compassion, fairness, peace, and respect for human dignity. The following selection of texts helps us to learn what God has to say concerning politics, government, and the state.

Genesis 4:15. By establishing the "mark of Cain," God initiated the institution of civil government.

Exodus 1:15-21. God praises and rewards the civil disobedience of the Hebrew midwives.

Exodus 1:22–2:10. The parents of Moses practice civil disobedience.

Exodus 3:10. "So now, go. I am sending you to Pharaoh to bring my people the Israelites out of Egypt." God orders Moses to lobby the top political ruler.

Exodus 3:18. God instructs the elders of Israel to lobby the king of Egypt.

Exodus 6:1. God controls the actions of the ungodly ruler, Pharaoh.

Exodus 8:28. Pharaoh acknowledges God and asks Moses to pray for him.

Exodus 9:27-28. Pharaoh acknowledges his sin, acknowledges that "the LORD is in the right," and requests prayer.

Exodus 10:10-11. Pharaoh acknowledges the Lord and the Lord's power.

Exodus 12:31-32. Pharaoh urges the Israelites to "worship the LORD" and requests a personal blessing.

Exodus 15:3. During the exodus, Moses and the Israelites declare that "the LORD is a warrior."

Exodus 15:14-18. The Lord reigns over all nations; they will hear him and tremble.

Exodus 17:8-16. God directs the Israelites under Joshua to fight the Amalekites while Moses prays.

Exodus 18:15-26. Moses lists the qualities required of godly judges.

Exodus 22:28. "Do not blaspheme God or curse the ruler of your people." The office of a political ruler is a high one, affirmed by God.

Exodus 23:1-9. Guidelines of justice and mercy for judges and political leaders are spelled out.

Leviticus 19:15. Justice is not to be perverted or partiality shown.

Deuteronomy 8:18-20. God judges even non-godly nations. He says that those nations that do not honor and obey him will be destroyed.

Deuteronomy 10:17-20. Godly guidelines for public policies are found here.

Deuteronomy 15:3-11. The needs of the poor must be met and foreign debt should be avoided.

Deuteronomy 17:8-13. Godly people must respect courts and judges. God will punish disrespect. (See also Exodus 22:28.)

Deuteronomy 17:14-20. God sets standards for kings and, by implication, for all who rule.

Judges 21:25. Absence of government creates anarchy.

1 Samuel 8:1-22. God respects the wishes of the Israelites to have a king and helps them choose Saul, although God does not approve of such action. (See also 1 Samuel 9:15-17; 12:17-19; and Hosea 13:11: "So in my anger I gave you a king, and in my wrath I took him away.")

2 Samuel 23:3. Rulers who rule over people with righteousness and "in the fear of God" please God.

1 Chronicles 22:6-10. Because David had been a warrior and had shed blood, he was not allowed to build God's temple.

1 Chronicles 28:3. Because David had been a warrior he could not build the temple, even though God had directed him to undertake such warfare (see 1 Samuel 23:2; and 2 Samuel 5:17-20). Warfare always brings with it much that is evil.

2 Chronicles 20:6. The Lord God rules "over all the kingdoms of the nations."

Ezra 6:10. The people shall "pray for the well-being of the king and his sons."

Nehemiah 9:2. "Those of Israelite descent . . . confessed their sins and the iniquities of their fathers." There is a place for collective apologies, even for past wrongs.

Esther 4:14; 5:1-8. Esther undertakes successful lobbying of King Xerxes.

Psalm 2:1-5. God laughs at and rebukes kings and rulers who oppose him, the Lord of all.

Psalm 2:10-11. Rulers are warned to serve the Lord with fear and trembling. They are accountable to God.

Psalm 9:15-20. A just God will punish all nations that forget him.

Psalm 11:7. The Lord is righteous and loves justice.

Psalm 22:27-28. Dominion belongs to the Lord, who rules over all the nations.

Psalm 33:10. "And with a breath he can scatter the plans of all nations who oppose him" (TLB).

Psalm 33:12. "Blessed is the nation whose God is the LORD." (See also verses 10-11.)

Psalm 46:8-9. "He makes wars cease to the ends of the earth; he breaks the bow and shatters the spear." (See also verse 10: "I will be exalted among the nations.")

Psalm 47:7-9. "God reigns over the nations . . . for the kings of the earth belong to God."

Psalm 66:7. God's "eyes watch the nations."

Psalm 72:8. "He shall have dominion also from sea to sea" (KJV). (This is the motto inscribed on Canada's Parliament buildings, with the word *also* deleted. See also 1-20.)

Psalm 82:3-4. God defends "the cause of the weak and fatherless," maintains "the rights of the poor and oppressed," and rescues "the weak and needy."

Psalm 86:9. "All the nations you have made will come and worship you."

Psalm 94:10. "Does he who disciplines nations not punish?"

Psalm 94:20. "Can a corrupt throne be allied with you—one that brings on misery by its decrees?"

Psalm 99:4. God loves justice and equity. (See also verses 1-2: "The Lord reigns, let the nations tremble.")

Psalm 102:15-20. "The nations will fear the name of the LORD, all the kings of the earth will revere your glory."

Psalm 110:6. "He will judge the nations, heaping up the dead and crushing the rulers of the whole earth."

Psalm 122:6. "Pray for the peace of Jerusalem."

Psalm 148:11-13. "Kings of the earth and all nations, you princes and rulers on earth . . . Let them praise the name of the LORD, for his name alone is exalted."

Proverbs 8:15-16. "By me kings reign and rulers make laws

that are just; by me princes govern and all nobles who rule on earth."

Proverbs 14:31. "He who oppresses the poor shows contempt for their Maker, but whoever is kind to the needy honors God."

Proverbs 14:34. "Righteousness exalts a nation, but sin is a disgrace to any people." (See also 16:12-15.)

Proverbs 17:15. "Acquitting the guilty and condemning the innocent—the LORD detests them both." (See also verses 23,26.)

Proverbs 21:1. "The king's heart is in the hand of the LORD; he directs it like a watercourse wherever he pleases."

Proverbs 22:22. "Do not exploit the poor because they are poor and do not crush the needy in court."

Proverbs 24:6. "For waging war you need guidance, and for victory many advisors." (See also 20:18.)

Proverbs 24:21. "Fear the LORD and the king, my son, and do not join with the rebellious."

Proverbs 24:23-25. "To show partiality in judging is not good; whoever says to the guilty, 'You are innocent'— peoples will curse him and nations denounce him. But it will go well with those who convict the guilty, and rich blessing will come upon them."

Proverbs 25:15. "Through patience a ruler can be persuaded."

Proverbs 28:9. "If anyone turns a deaf ear to the law, even his prayers are detestable."

Proverbs 29:4. "By justice a king gives a country stability, but one who is greedy for bribes tears it down."

Proverbs 29:7. "The righteous care about justice for the poor." (See also verse 26.)

Proverbs 31:8-9. Godly people shall speak up to defend the rights of the poor and those who cannot speak for themselves.

Ecclesiastes 3:8. There is "a time for war and a time for peace."

Ecclesiastes 10:2. "The heart of the wise inclines to the right, but the heart of the fool to the left." (This verse is often misused. Compare Isaiah 30:21 as well as Proverbs 4:27: "Do not swerve to the right or the left.")

Isaiah 1:17. "Seek justice, encourage the oppressed. Defend the cause of the fatherless, plead the case of the widow."

Isaiah 1:23. Rulers are condemned for loving bribes and chasing after gifts.

Isaiah 10:1-2. "Woe to those who make unjust laws, to those who issue oppressive decrees, to deprive the poor of their rights and withhold justice from the oppressed of my people."

Isaiah 10:5-11. God uses evil governments as his agents.

Isaiah 13:1-5. God uses military forces to achieve his goals. (See also 13:17-20.)

Isaiah 14:24-27. God will crush the Assyrian regime because of its oppression. God has a "plan determined for the whole world; this is the hand stretched out over all nations." (For detailed prophecies against various cities and nations, see also Isaiah 14:28-29; chapters 15–24.)

Isaiah 34:1-3. Because of their evil actions, "the LORD is angry with all nations."

Isaiah 40:23. "He brings princes to naught and reduces the rulers of this world to nothing."

Isaiah 42:1-4. God gives an emphatic and repeated call for justice.

Isaiah 44:28—45:4. God uses an unbeliever, King Cyrus, to achieve his ends.

Isaiah 45:4-5. God bestows a title of honor on King Cyrus, a pagan ruler.

Isaiah 59:8. Through his prophet Isaiah, God accuses Israel of not knowing the way of peace and justice.

Isaiah 59:14-16. When there is no justice, the Lord wants someone to intercede.

Isaiah 61:1-11. God calls for enlightened, positive, and accountable public policy.

Jeremiah 5:28. It is wrong not to "plead the case of the fatherless" and not to "defend the rights of the poor."

Jeremiah 25:7-14. Because of the evil in Judah, God will use the king of Babylon, "my servant Nebuchadnezzar," to punish God's own people. (See also 27:4-7.)

Jeremiah 29:7. "Seek the peace and prosperity of the city to which I have carried you."

Lamentations 3:35-36. "To deny a man his rights before the Most High, to deprive a man of justice—would not the Lord see such things?" They are obviously evil!

Ezekiel 34:4. Caring for the weak is a good policy for rulers.

Daniel 3:1-30. Shadrach, Meshach, and Abednego practice civil disobedience and are eventually praised by King Nebuchadnezzar.

Daniel 4:31-33. God is sovereign over all kingdoms and holds even non-believing rulers accountable.

Daniel 4:34-37. An ungodly ruler eventually praises God for his enduring kingdom and justice.

Daniel 5:22-30. God punishes ungodly Belshazzar for not honoring God, who holds in his hand Belshazzar's life and all his ways.

Daniel 6:1-5. Daniel serves as a totally honest, competent, and incorruptible senior government official.

Daniel 6:8-23. Daniel practices civil disobedience and is rescued from the lions' den.

Joel 3:2. "I will gather all nations and . . . enter into judgment against them." (See also Jeremiah 21:11–23:6.)

Amos 1:1-15. God will punish pagan rulers for their wrong deeds. (See also other passages in chapters 1–2 for the specific sins of cities and countries.)

Amos 5:12, 15. "For I know how many are your offenses. . . . You oppress the righteous and take bribes and you deprive the poor of justice in the courts. . . . Hate evil, love good: maintain justice in the courts."

Amos 5:24. "But let justice roll on like a river, righteousness like a never-failing stream!"

Amos 6:14. "For the LORD God Almighty declares, 'I will stir up a nation against you.'"

Amos 9:8. "Surely the eyes of the Sovereign LORD are on the sinful kingdom. I will destroy it."

Obadiah 1:15. "The day of the LORD is near for all nations. As you have done, it will be done to you."

Micah 7:3. God condemns the ruler who "demands gifts" and the judge who "accepts bribes."

Habakkuk 1:5-11. God uses even pagan rulers and nations in mighty ways. They come under his power.

Habakkuk 2:12. "Woe to him who builds a city with bloodshed and establishes a town by crime!"

Zephaniah 3:1. "Woe to the city of oppressors."

Matthew 2:7-12. The Magi are instructed by God to practice civil disobedience.

Matthew 5:44. "Love your enemies and pray for those who persecute you." (See also Luke 6:27-31.)

Matthew 8:5-13. Jesus commends the military commander, a centurion, for his exceptionally great faith.

Matthew 14:3-4. Although a prisoner, John the Baptist challenges Herod, the ruler, because of his sin.

Matthew 17:24-27. Jesus approves the payment of local temple taxes.

Matthew 22:15-22. Jesus approves the payment of taxes to Caesar. (See also Mark 12:13-17; Luke 20:20-26.)

Matthew 22:37-39. Loving one's neighbor is extremely important. This practice has both personal and social dimensions. (See also Mark 12:28-31; Luke 10:27.)

Matthew 25:31-46. Jesus describes God-pleasing social behavior and thus also social policies.

Matthew 27:22-26. By inference, this description from Jesus' sentencing denounces political opportunism that, in this case, resulted in gross miscarriage of justice. (See also Luke 23:13-24; John 19:2-16.)

Mark 6:14-29. John the Baptist challenges King Herod concerning his immorality, then Queen Herodias manages to have John the Baptist beheaded.

Luke 3:12-13. John the Baptist instructs tax collectors to be honest in their tax collection.

Luke 3:14. John the Baptist instructs soldiers not to extort money, not to accuse people falsely, and to be content with their wages.

Luke 4:5-7. The devil asserts that he controls "all the kingdoms of the world."

Luke 7:1-10. Luke describes the exceptional and praiseworthy faith of a military officer.

Luke 11:42. Leaders who neglect justice are condemned.

Luke 14:31-32. Earthly kings do go to war; Jesus notes some basic elements of military planning.

Luke 17:20-21. "The kingdom of God is within you."

Luke 18:18-27. Jesus gives some hard advice to a rich ruler.

Luke 19:1-10. Zacchaeus can, as a believer, work as a tax collector if he is honest.

Luke 23:50-53. In a case of gentle lobbying, Joseph of Arimathea asks for a favor from Pilate, the ruler.

John 18:36. Jesus says, "My kingdom is not of this world. If it were, my servants would fight to prevent my arrest."

John 19:10-12. Jesus tells Pilate that he would have no power "if it were not given to you from above."

Acts 4:18-21. Some apostles courageously practice civil disobedience by preaching.

Acts 5:25-29. Peter and other apostles explain the reason for their civil disobedience: "We must obey God rather than men!"

Acts 5:33-42. Gamaliel was a wise and just man serving in civil government.

Acts 9:15. Paul is commissioned by God to witness to kings.

Acts 13:7-12. A key political leader, the proconsul Sergius Paulus, sends for Barnabas and Saul because he wants to hear the gospel. Paul witnesses to him and he becomes a Christian.

Acts 16:37-39. Paul and Silas claim citizenship rights. Paul presses civil authorities to treat him fairly.

Acts 21:30-32. Government soldiers stop a riot; they maintain law and order.

Acts 22:25-29. Paul claims citizenship rights.

Acts 22:30. Government officials rely on religious leaders for help.

Acts 23:10. Military troops rescue Paul.

Acts 23:17-24. Paul seeks the help of a military officer. A military officer dispatches 470 soldiers to protect Paul.

Acts 23:25-29. A military commander writes a reference letter for Paul.

Acts 24:10-26. Paul testifies before Governor Felix as well as to him.

Acts 25:8-12. Paul invokes his citizenship rights and appeals to the court of Caesar in Rome.

Acts 25:13-21. Governor Felix acts wisely, following a high ethic.

Acts 25:22—26:32. Paul, as a prisoner, witnesses to King Agrippa.

Acts 28:19. Paul explains that he "was compelled to appeal to Caesar."

Romans 13:1-7. The political authorities have been established by God; they are his servants and agents and have specific roles. Christians should respect and honor them and pay their taxes.

Romans 14:17-18. Paul gives a description of the kingdom of God.

1 Corinthians 2:6-8. There is a great difference between Christian wisdom and the wisdom of "the rulers of this age."

2 Corinthians 3:17. "Where the Spirit of the Lord is, there is freedom."

2 Corinthians 10:3. "For though we live in the world, we do not wage war as the world does."

Galatians 5:1. "It is for freedom that Christ has set us free." (See also verse 13.)

Philippians 3:20. The citizenship of Christians "is in heaven."

Philippians 4:21-22. There were Christian saints in Caesar's household.

Colossians 1:16. God has created all thrones, powers, rulers, and authorities.

Colossians 2:10. Christ "is the head over every power and authority."

1 Timothy 2:1-2. "I urge, then, first of all, that requests, prayers, intercession and thanksgiving be made for everyone—for kings and all those in authority."

1 Timothy 6:15. The Lord Jesus Christ is the "King of kings and Lord of lords."

2 Timothy 2:2-4. This is an apparently favorable reference to soldiers.

Titus 3:1-2. Christians are reminded to be subject to rulers and authorities.

James 2:12. God's law produces freedom.

1 Peter 2:13-14. Christians shall submit themselves, for the Lord's sake, to kings, authorities, and governors. Christians are to honor the king, who has been given tasks by God.

1 Peter 2:16. "Live as free men, but do not use your freedom as a cover-up for evil."

1 Peter 3:22. All "authorities and powers [are] in submission to" Jesus Christ, "who has gone into heaven."

Revelation 1:5. Jesus Christ is "the ruler of the kings of the earth."

Revelation 1:6. This is a comment about the spiritual kingdom of God.

Revelation 18:1-24. God judges Babylon; it is doomed because of its evil deeds. This indicates that God has standards for rulers and empires and that God evaluates them.

Notes

Introduction

John Howard Yoder, *The Politics of Jesus* (Grand Rapids: Eerdmans, 1972), 144.

Chapter 2

1. "On Secular Authority," *Works of Martin Luther,* vol. 3 (Philadelphia: Muhlenberg, 1930), 236.

2. Thomas G. Sanders, *Protestant Concepts of Church and State* (New York: Holt, Rinehart and Winston, 1964), 34.

3. Sanders, 34.

4. *Works of Martin Luther,* 241.

5. Ibid., 269-70.

6. Sanders, 39.

7. Wilhelm Niesel, *The Theology of Calvin* (Philadelphia: Westminster, 1936), 230.

8. Sanders, 227.

9. John Calvin, *Institutes,* 4.20.2.

10. Sanders, 227.

11. Calvin, 4.20.2.

12. Ibid., 4.20.9.

13. Sanders, 231.

Chapter 3

1. Sanders, 75.

2. Ibid., 109.

3. Ibid., 47.

4. Ibid., 92

5. *The Schleitheim Confession,* art. 6 (Kitchener, ON, and Scottdale, PA: Herald Press, 1977), 15.

6. See, for example, John H. Redekop, "Decades of transition: North American Mennonite Brethren in Politics" in Paul Toews, ed., *Bridging Troubled Waters: The Mennonite Brethren at Mid-Twentieth Century* (Winnipeg, MB: Kindred Press, 1995), 19-84.

Chapter 6

1. For an account of a Christian-American movement and an analysis of the entire phenomenon, see John H. Redekop, *The American Far Right: A Case Study of Billy James Hargis and Christian Crusade* (Grand Rapids, MI: Eerdmans, 1968).

2. For my initial column, see "Merchants of Death," *Mennonite Brethren Herald,* September 30, 1985, 15. For the *Toronto Star* news account, see "Mennonite criticizes plan to push tobacco," *Toronto Star,* October 8, 1985. Other newspapers also carried this news item.

Chapter 11

1. Daniel B. Stevick, *Civil Disobedience and the Christian,* (New York: The Seabury Press, 1969), 119.

Conclusion

1. As quoted in "A change of heart; Billy Graham on the nuclear arms race." *The Christian Leader,* August 1979, 5.

2. "Christian America," *Kitchener-Waterloo Record,* January 4, 1986, B3.

3. Richard John Neuhaus, *The Naked Public Square: Religion and Democracy in America* (Grand Rapids, MI: Eerdmans, 1984), 122.

4. Ibid., 120.

Index

Aaron, 90
absolute claims, 85
advising governments, 152-53
Agrippa, King, 107, 191, 199
Americans United for
  Separation of Church and
  State, 19
Anabaptist Realism, 19, 23
Anabaptists, 18, 55-56, 57f.
  an evaluation, 66-67, 89
  as alternative society, 63
  avoidance of politics, 65,
  128
  later modifications, 67-68
  on brotherhood, 61
  on church-state relations, 61,
  63-67
  on government office, 58
  on military service, 65
  on religious freedom, 64
  on separation of church
  and state, 64
  on voluntarism, 59, 61
  one ethic, 21, 59f., 65, 88-89
  pacifism, 62
  persecution, 60, 63
  role of the state, 64
  "the quiet in the land," 66

the two covenants, 62
  view of Scripture, 22, 58, 61
anarchy, 32, 35, 39, 74, 98,
  105, 199, 202
Aquinas, Thomas, 17

Belshazzar, King, 54, 81, 199
benefiting from government,
  129-30, 134f.
big government, 98, 115
  a mixed record, 127
  expansion, 127-28
  response to, 128, 138
Blair, Tony, 110
Brown v. Board of Education
  1954, 142
Buddhism, 194
Burke, Edmund, 125

Caesar, 30, 32, 42, 105, 202
Calvin, John, 18, 50f., 57-58,
  59, 60
  an evaluation, 53-54
  and Anabaptists, 62-63
  execution of dissenters, 52
  on ethical dualism, 92
  role of the state, 51f.
  two orders, 19

The Author

John H. Redekop is the author of three books, including *The American Far Right* (1968) and *A People Apart: Ethnicity and the Mennonite Brethren* (1987). He has edited three books of essays and authored scores of articles on public policy. For many years he was a panelist on the Canadian TV show *Cross Currents* and its predecessor, *The Stiller Report*. From 1991 to 1993 he was president of the Evangelical Fellowship of Canada. Redekop was professor of political science at Wilfrid Laurier University and at Trinity Western University. He was elected city counselor in Abbotsford, British Columbia, in 1999 and served until 2002. Redekop was born in Herbert, Saskatchewan.